BEADED
COLLARS

BEADED
COLLARS

*10 Decorative Neckpieces
Built with Ladder Stitch*

Julia S. Pretl

Creative Publishing
international

Creative Publishing
international

Copyright © 2007 Julia S. Pretl
Creative Publishing international, Inc.
400 First Avenue North
Suite 300
Minneapolis, MN 55401
1-800-328-3895
www.creativepub.com

ISBN-13: 978-1-58923-381-2
ISBN-10: 1-58923-381-6

10 9 8 7 6 5 4 3 2 1

Library of Congress Cataloging-in-Publication Data
Pretl, Julia S.
  Beaded collars : 10 decorative neckpieces built with ladder stitch / Julia S. Pretl.
      p. cm.
  Includes index.
  ISBN 1-58923-381-6
  1. Beadwork--Patterns. 2. Necklaces. I. Title.
  TT860.P73 2008
  745.58'2--dc22

                                        2007034505
                                           CIP

Cover Design: Dawn S. Sokol
Book Design: Silke Braun
Page Layout: Silke Braun
Illustrations: Julia S. Pretl
Technical Editor: Judith Durant

Printed in China

Dedication

Dedicated to Deborah Cannarella and Judith Durant, who not only helped to make this book possible, but made it enjoyable as well.

Thank you both.

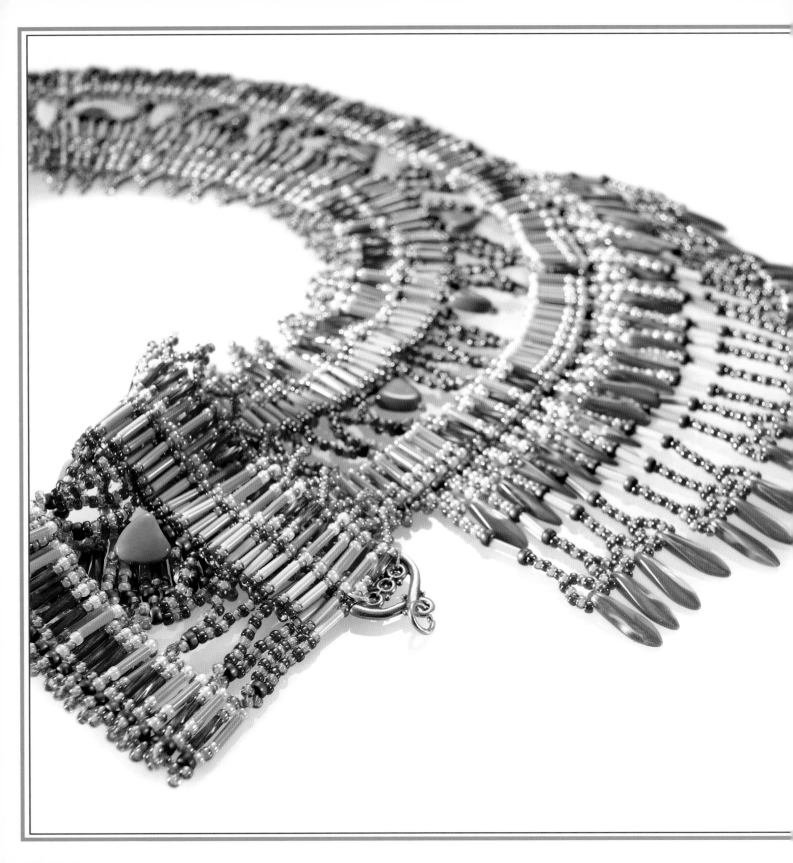

Contents

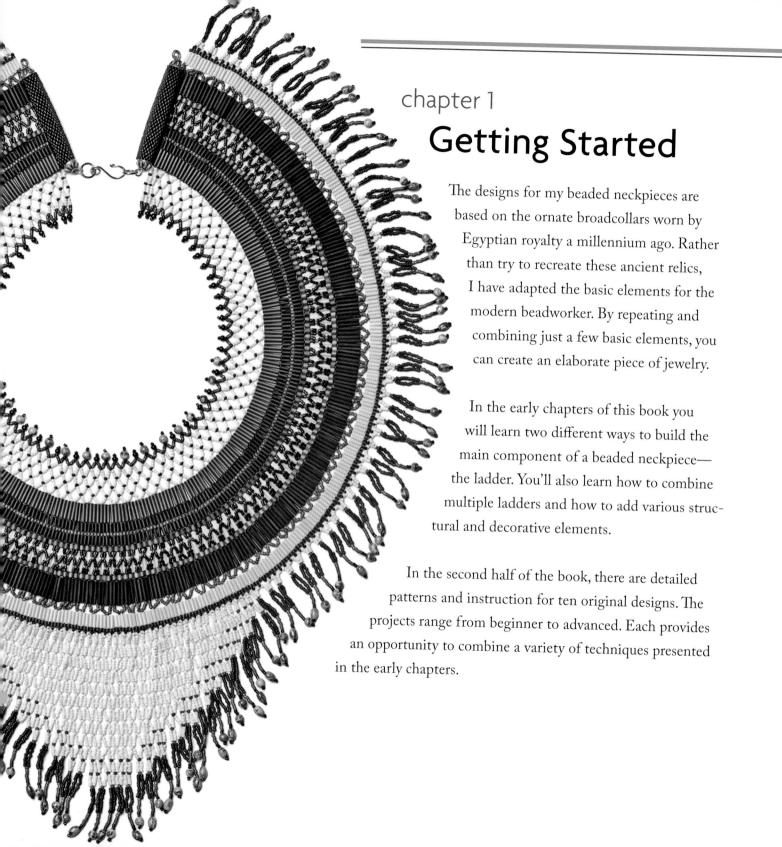

chapter 1
Getting Started

The designs for my beaded neckpieces are based on the ornate broadcollars worn by Egyptian royalty a millennium ago. Rather than try to recreate these ancient relics, I have adapted the basic elements for the modern beadworker. By repeating and combining just a few basic elements, you can create an elaborate piece of jewelry.

In the early chapters of this book you will learn two different ways to build the main component of a beaded neckpiece—the ladder. You'll also learn how to combine multiple ladders and how to add various structural and decorative elements.

In the second half of the book, there are detailed patterns and instruction for ten original designs. The projects range from beginner to advanced. Each provides an opportunity to combine a variety of techniques presented in the early chapters.

MATERIALS AND SUPPLIES

To make these beaded neckpieces, you will need the following materials and supplies. Each project includes a materials list with the specific materials for that project. Because correct sizing is so important, I have also provided the amount of beads you will need for each size in the range of sizes provided.

- Size 12 or smaller beading needles
- Strong bead thread (I use either 16 lb GSP fishing line or size 46 bonded nylon)
- Thin, sharp pins with a glass or plastic ball at the top
- Sharp, fine tipped scissors
- Tape measure with metric units
- Ruler with metric units
- Compass with metric units
- Calculator
- White paper, 8½"× 8½" (20.3 × 20.3 cm) or larger
- Foam board or a flat, sturdy cardboard box, 14" x 14" (35.5 × 35.5 cm) or larger
- Mechanical pencil for marking the template

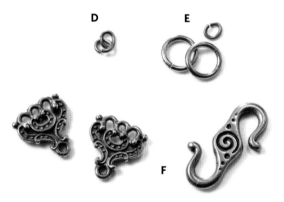

A 6mm × 2mm and 12mm × 2mm bugle beads
B 11° and 8° seed beads
C Dagger beads, crystals, stone chips, and other decorative beads
D 1.5cm to 3cm multistrand necklace reducers
E Jump rings
F Clasps or S hooks

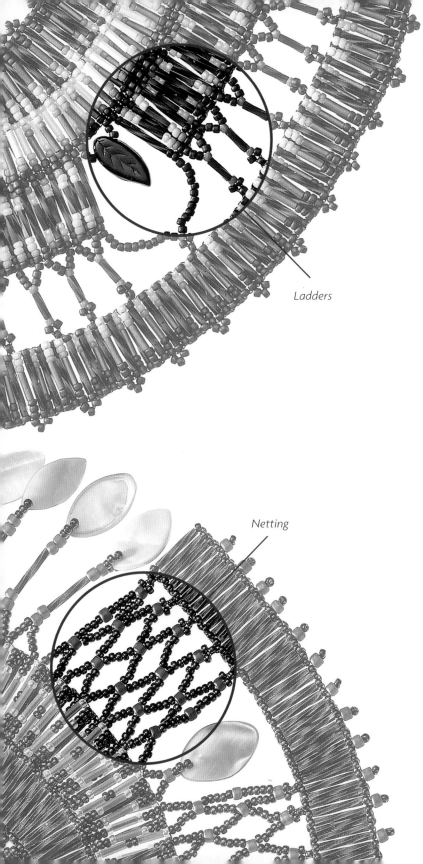

Ladders

Netting

ELEMENTS OF A BEADED NECKPIECE

When you make a beaded neckpiece, you have the creative freedom to combine several basic elements to make a unique design. You don't need to include every element in every collar, however. Here are some of the many elements you can choose from.

Ladders

Ladders make up the framework of the beaded neckpiece. A single ladder is made of multiple "bead units," each of which includes at least one bugle bead and at least one 11° seed bead on either end (to buffer the thread from the sharp edges of the bugle bead). You sew the units together, side by side, to make a long dense ribbon of beads. Then you pin the ladders to a template and join them to form circles. This concentric formation allows the neckpiece to hold its shape when you remove it from the template.

Netting

Netting is used to join ladders, and it also creates open areas, which provide visual interest in the design. You can create a light, airy feel by beading a row of netting between each ladder. Or you can add rows more sparingly—even a single row of netting will provide interesting contrast to the otherwise dense structure of several consecutive ladder rows. Your netting can be very complex and intricate, as in Trellis on page 103. Or it can be as simple as single spokes that span from one ladder to the next, as in Drab on page 57. Netted rows may include bugle beads, seed beads of varying sizes, crystals, pressed glass, or any other number of decorative elements.

Layering

In most cases, you will add new elements of the design to the edges of existing elements. You can, however, also work on the surface of your neckpiece to build layers, which will add depth and texture. One way to do this is by netting from the outside edge of a ladder to the inside edge of another, spanning one or more ladders in between.

Surface Embellishment

Surface embellishments add extra dimension to your beadwork, and sewing is a simple way to adorn the surface. Just stitch beads, pressed glass flowers, stone chips, or any other decoration at the juncture of two ladders. It's easiest to add these elements while you are weaving in and out of a ladder to join a subsequent row.

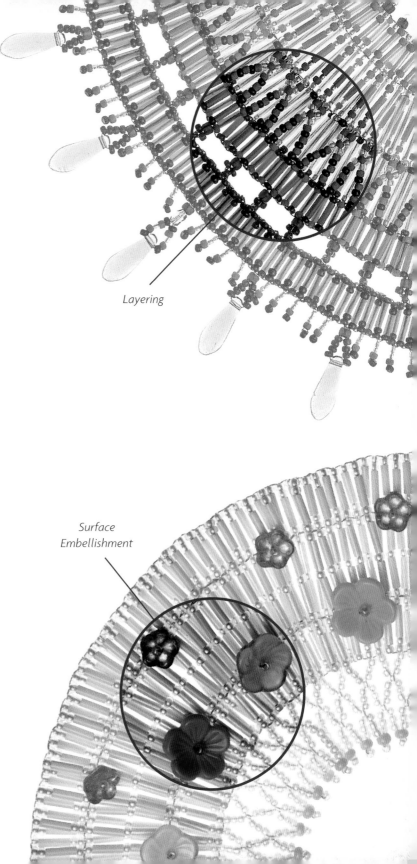

Layering

Surface Embellishment

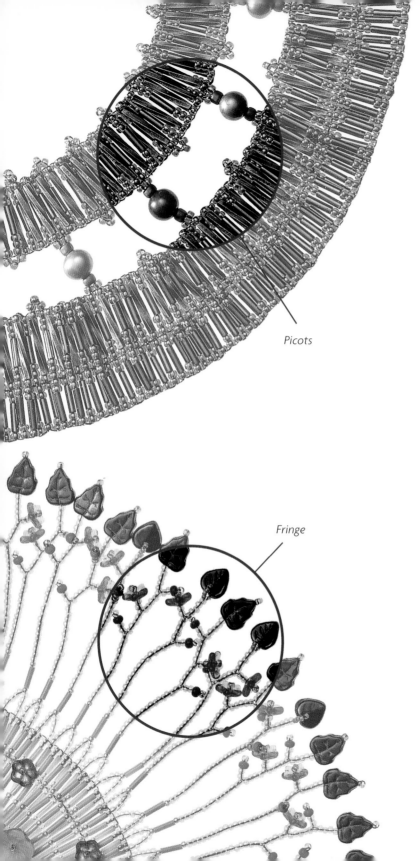

Picots

Fringe

Picots

Picots are small beaded loops along a beaded edge. Small picots, usually made with one to three beads, add texture to the straight edges of the beaded ladders. Most often, you'll add picots to the innermost or top ladder. You can also add them to the outer edge, within netted segments, or anywhere else within the neckpiece that you'd like extra embellishment.

Fringe

Fringe is basically an extended picot. Fringe adds drama and fluidity to the piece. You can create fringe that is long and straight, branched, looped, or layered. If you add daggers or other large beads along the bottoms of the strands, the fringe will sway with the wearer's every movement.

Closures

You'll add a closure to the back of each end of the neckpiece to clasp the neckpiece shut. You'll also add a metal finding to which you'll attach each closure. The metal findings should be broad enough to span at least one row (usually the initial ladder) to accommodate the weight of the neckpiece. Be sure they are securely attached. Metal reducers, which are often used for multistrand necklaces, are ideal findings for these projects.

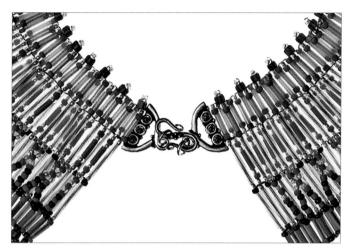

Closures

Counterweights

Some neckpieces are asymmetrical from front to back—in other words, they may be heavier at the front, either by design or because there is a large amount of heavy fringe. To properly balance the neckpiece, you may need to add a counterweight at the back. A decorative coin with a center hole, a smooth stone decorated with beads, or a fishing weight are some of the many types of objects that work well as counterweights.

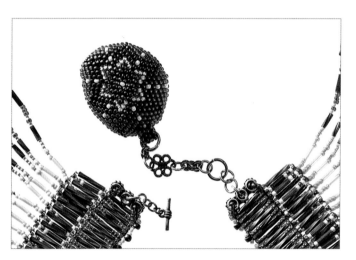

Counterweights

MEASURING AND MAKING A TEMPLATE

The first step to making a beaded neckpiece is to create a template. The template serves as the workspace on which you will secure your first row of beads, make measurements, add further rows, and make notations that will help you determine where to join additional elements.

Measuring for Circumference

Measure the base of your neck with a metric tape measure to find your neck circumference. The neckpiece will lie flat on your shoulders and breast plate, so be sure you measure your neck where it meets your body—not any higher. Add 2 cm to the measurement to allow for a comfortable fit. The total is the circumference of the first, innermost ladder of your neckpiece.

Now divide that number to find the diameter and then the radius of the circumference. You will then set your compass to the radius dimension to make the correct-size circle on your template. Here's the formula:

___ (circumference + 2 cm) ÷ 3.14 = ___ (diameter)

___ (diameter) ÷ 2 = ___ (radius)

Record and label each of these measurements. Metric measurements are standard for measuring beads, so you'll work with metric measurements throughout this book. You'll find it much easier to stick with metric than to convert millimeters to inches as you work.

Making the Template

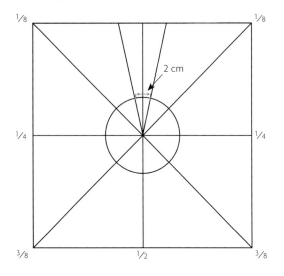

Before setting up your workspace, you need to prepare the template by drawing a few essential guidelines. It is important that your template is as square as possible so that these guidelines are accurate. Begin with a square sheet of paper that is at least 8½" x 8½" (21.6 × 21.6 cm).

Measure and mark the halfway point of each of the four edges of the square. Draw lines to connect the marks on opposite sides so that the paper is divided into four smaller squares. These lines will serve as markers as you create your neckpiece: the horizontal line is the ¼ marker, and the vertical line is the ½ marker.

Now draw a line from one corner of the square to the opposite corner. Repeat to connect the other two corners. These lines will serve as ⅜ markers. Your paper is now divided into eight triangles.

Set your compass to the radius you computed in the formula above. Place the point of the compass at the center of the template (where all four lines intersect). Draw a circle. The measurement of each line within the circle should be equal to the diameter in your formula.

Make two marks on either side of the vertical line that intersects the top edge of the circle. Each mark should be 1 cm from the line. You will leave the area between the marks free of beads so you can add the clasp there.

With tape or glue, adhere the template to the center of a sheet of foam board or a flat cardboard box. Now you have your work surface.

CHOOSING BEADS AND COLORS

The next step is to decide what the ladders will look like. There are only two rules you need to remember:

1. Every bugle bead must have a seed bead on each end.

2. Every bead unit within one ladder must be the same height.

Experiment with different combinations of beads. Stack them on straight pins and stand the pins side by side on your work surface. Think about the effect that you want to achieve. Do you want subtle colors that graduate from light to dark? Or do you want strong contrast in the colors of one unit and the next—or possibly even within one bead unit? Do you want every unit to be the same or do you want to create a rhythmic patterning with the ladder? How many different combinations do you want within a single ladder?

The drawings below show the combinations in the designs for the projects in this book. Refer to them as you think about the qualities you would like to have in your own designs.

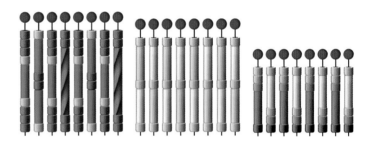

When you have finished experimenting, save the combinations that you like by making a "swatch library" of short ladders. Then work with these swatches to decide how you would like to combine the colors and the ladders. Once you've decided on several combinations you like, you're ready to begin making the long ladders for your neckpiece.

chapter 2
Making Ladders

The ladders are the foundation of the neckpiece. They hold the piece together and, once they are joined, they give the piece its final shape and structure. You can build ladders with either the one-needle or the two-needle method. The main difference is in the way you string the beads. The resulting ladders are identical, so the method you choose is simply a matter of preference.

When building a ladder, the order in which you string the beads is important. With the one-needle technique, you will string a large number of beads before constructing the ladder. With the two-needle technique, you will add bead units one at a time and build the ladder gradually. Regardless of the technique you choose, you must always string the bead units from top to bottom and then from bottom to top, so the pattern is correct.

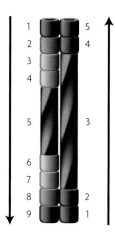

ONE-NEEDLE METHOD

String the beads for your first ladder in the correct order, as determined by your swatch library or as indicated in the instructions for the specific project you're making.

Begin with a piece of thread about 10' (3 m) long. To get the length you need, simply pull the thread from the spool twice, stretching your arms to their full length and measuring each length from fingertip to fingertip.

Thread a needle at one end and make a "stopper bead" by picking up a seed bead and sliding it to the center of your thread. Sew through this bead once more, making sure not to pierce the thread. The stopper bead should move back and forth along the thread with little effort, but the friction of the thread loop around the bead will keep it from moving too freely, keeping all the other beads from falling off the thread.

Referring to your sample swatch or the project instructions, string your first bead unit in order from bottom to top and string the second unit in order from top to bottom.

Continue to string beads this way until there are about 18" (46 cm) of thread remaining from the last bead to the needle. Slide the stopper bead so that it is about 18" (46 cm) from the far end of the thread. Slide the strung bead units to meet it, as shown in top drawing below.

Slide the first two bead units so that they are about two finger widths from the rest of the beads. Skip the first bead unit and sew into the far end of the second unit. The two units will fold the shared length of thread in half, causing the length of the second bead unit to lay parallel atop the length of the first bead unit, as shown in the bottom two drawings.

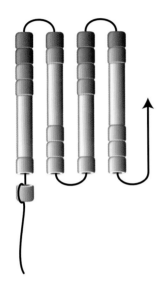

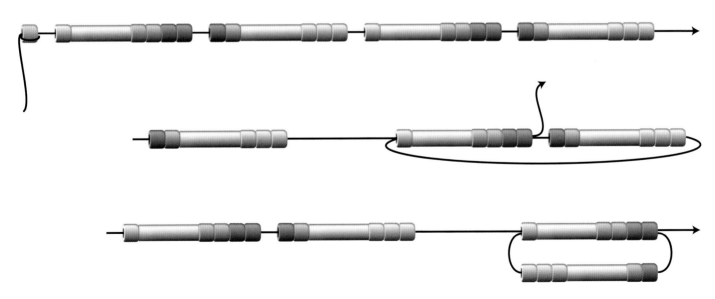

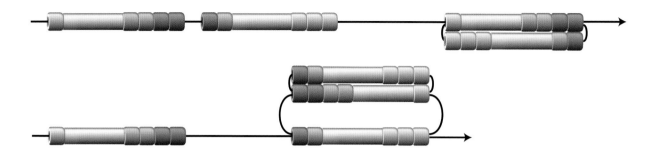

Pull the thread taut so that the first two units sit one above the next, as shown in the top drawing above.

Slide the next bead unit forward and sew into the far end of this unit. Pull taut, once again folding the shared thread in half. You should now have three parallel bead units, as shown in the bottom drawing above.

After joining several units, you will find that you are not able to slide any more bead units forward. When you reach this point, allow more space by sliding the stopper bead several inches along the thread.

Repeat the process and continue to build the ladder until there are 6" to 8" (15 to 20 cm) of thread free at each end.

TWO-NEEDLE METHOD

Begin with a piece of thread about 10' (3 m) long. To get the length you need, simply pull the thread from the spool twice, stretching your arms to their full length and measuring each length from fingertip to fingertip.

Add a needle to each end of the thread. String your first bead unit in order from top to bottom. String the second unit in order from bottom to top. Slide both units to the center of the length of thread.

With the needle that comes out of the second bead unit, sew into the far end of the first bead unit and exit the last bead of the same unit. The two units will fold the shared length of thread in half.

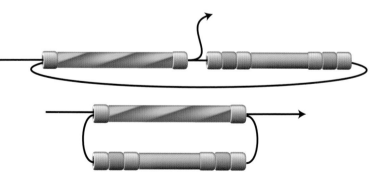

Pull the thread taut so that the first two units sit side by side.

Add a new bead unit, making sure to string the beads in the correct order. Sew into the far end of the new unit with the second needle and pull the thread taut.

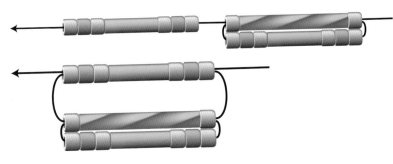

Repeat the process and continue to build the ladder until there are 6" to 8" (15 to 20 cm) of thread free at each end. You will need to end the ladder and then add more thread and beads to extend it to the length you want.

ENDING A LADDER

Before continuing the ladder, you need to tie off the thread extending from the ends of the top unit.

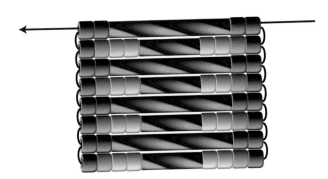

Remove the stopper bead from the end of the thread. If you are working with the one-needle method, you may find that several bead units remain on the thread, but the working end becomes too short to continue. Simply remove any remaining bead units. Sew into the next-to-last unit so that both thread ends are on the same side of the ladder.

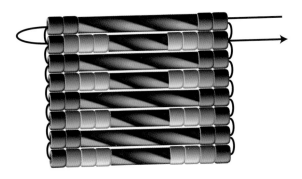

Secure the thread ends by tying them together twice, each time with an overhand knot. Pull the thread tight enough that the last two ladders do not separate—but not so tight that the end of the ladder buckles.

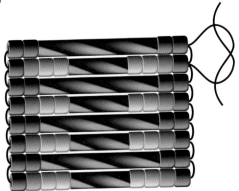

Remove the needle(s) and allow the thread ends to remain as they are. You will weave these ends into your work after the ladders are joined.

EXTENDING A LADDER

To extend a one-needle ladder, pull a new length of thread from your spool and, once again, "load" your thread so that half is strung with beads. Add the needle and sew through the last unit of your existing ladder, making sure to enter the proper side, as determined by your swatch or project instructions. Continue building the ladder until it is the desired length or until you run out of thread again.

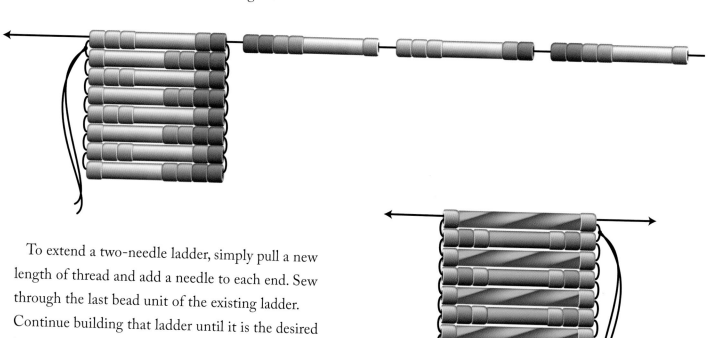

To extend a two-needle ladder, simply pull a new length of thread and add a needle to each end. Sew through the last bead unit of the existing ladder. Continue building that ladder until it is the desired length or until you run out of thread again.

ESTIMATING LADDER LENGTH

When planning your beaded neckpiece, it helps to know roughly how long each ladder needs to be. To estimate ladder length, you'll need to make a few simple calculations.

First you need to know the diameter of your neck opening. This is the diameter of the circle that you drew on your template. For subsequent ladders, measure the diameter of the circle from the outside edges of the outermost ladder (or points for netted rows) at the ¼-marker line on your template.

1. Find the circumference of the outer edge of the last row with this formula:

____ cm (diameter) x 3.14 = ____ cm (circumference)

This measurement is the circumference of the subsequent ladder.

2. Next you need to know how many bead units you need to span the circumference. One cm of the circle requires approximately 5.5 bead units.

____ cm (circumference) x 5.5 = ____ (units needed)

3. It's helpful to know the measurement of the ladder when it lies straight so you can estimate the length you'll need to have before you pin it to the template. One centimeter of a straight ladder requires approximately 4.7 bead units:

____ (units needed) ÷ 4.7 = ____ cm (straight ladder length)

Keep in mind that the ladder will be slightly shorter than your estimated length because you are leaving space free to accommodate the clasp.

You can get a more accurate estimate of the final length when the ladder is roughly halfway completed. Temporarily pin the ladder to the template from either clasp mark to the ½-marker line at the bottom of your template. Mark the halfway point on your ladder with a pin or a piece of string. Remove the ladder from the template. Lay the ladder straight and measure the distance from the beginning of the ladder to the halfway point. Multiply this number by two in order to find the total length you'll need.

chapter 3
Assembly

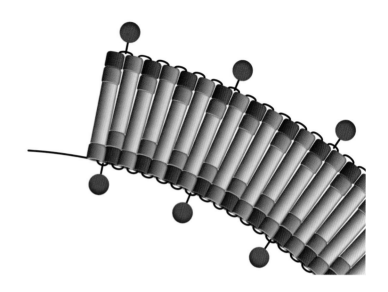

You only need to make one ladder at a time. When you have completed each ladder, you will pin it to the template and join it to the others. Once you begin designing your own neckpieces, however, you might want to make at least one segment of each ladder to help you plan the overall design.

PINNING LADDERS TO THE TEMPLATE

The first ladder is the most difficult to pin to the template because there are no other ladders to help you secure it. Carefully insert a straight pin through the small space at the inner (top) edge where the thread joins the first bead unit to the second bead unit. Make sure that you don't pierce the thread as this will weaken the ladder. Insert the pin into the template at one of the two marks that you made to accommodate the clasp.

Gently curve the ladder to conform to the shape of the circle, pinning both the inner and outer edges every couple of centimeters. Try not to stretch the outer edge of the ladder. Instead, allow the inner edge to rumple slightly, like a fan. Work all the way around to the second clasp mark.

You may need to readjust some of the pins to make sure that the bead units are evenly distributed.

The second and all subsequent ladders are considerably easier to pin to the template. Place the ladder on the template so that the first unit of the ladder is aligned with the first unit of the previous ladder—the idea is that they appear to be continuous units. Wrap the new ladder around the circle, pinning both edges enough to secure them, until you reach the opposite end. Readjust pins if necessary.

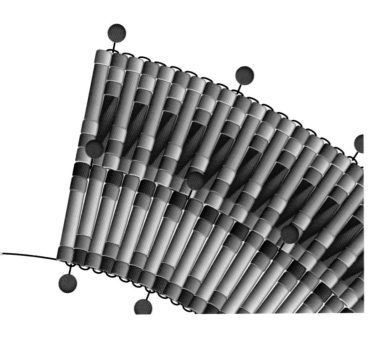

Each ladder in the project patterns contains more bead units than the preceding ladder in order to create concentric rings. As you join ladders, you'll see that each consecutive unit of the outer ladder is increasingly farther from the next unit of the inner ladder. With a bit of gentle manipulation, you can sew smoothly from one unit to the next, but eventually you will reach a point where you would have to stretch the outer ladder in order to meet the corresponding inner ladder. To keep the bead units evenly distributed without stretching the outer ladder, skip one bead unit in the outer ladder as you join it to the inner ladder. Make sure that you only skip one bead unit at a time to avoid leaving gaps in your beadwork.

JOINING THE FIRST TWO LADDERS

Now that you have pinned the second ladder to the template, you will join it to the first ladder. Begin by placing a stopper bead on a length of thread at least 5' (1.5 m) long. Thread a needle at one end. Sew through the outer edge of the first bead unit of the outermost ladder, then sew through the first unit of the previous ladder so that you exit the inside of the circle. Now work in the opposite direction, sewing through the second unit of each ladder until you exit the outer edge. Work back and forth in this way until you have joined several more units in each ladder.

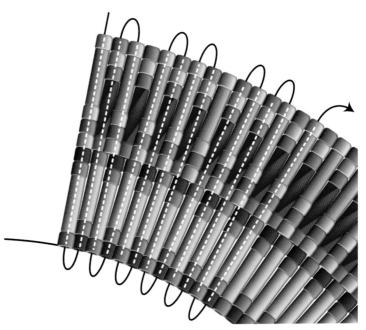

If you are unsure where in the ladder to skip a bead unit, make a "ray" to determine the best location. Place a straight pin at the center point of your template. Tie one end of a length of thread around the pin. Now lay the thread tautly across your neckpiece to find the most direct path from the unit of one ladder to a unit of the next.

ENDING AND BEGINNING THREADS

Eventually you will need to begin a new thread—usually when the thread you're working with is only about 6" (16 cm) long. Simply remove the needle and begin a new length of thread as before, adding a stopper bead and rethreading the needle. The ladders are secured to the template, so they'll stay in place even when the tension on the working thread is loose. Continue to join the ladders one unit at a time. When you have joined nine or ten units, the thread will be secure enough for you to remove the stopper bead and tie the two ends together with an overhand knot.

It's best to leave all thread ends hanging from your neckpiece until it is complete. This way, you won't clog a bead with doubled threads, which helps if you want to add elements through that bead later.

If you have so many hanging threads that it's hard to work, however, it's okay to finish some of them ahead of time—but only if you sew through bead units that you are positive you will not need later. Finish each loose end, one at a time, by weaving it through two or three bead units. Then cut the thread close to the beadwork with sharp scissors.

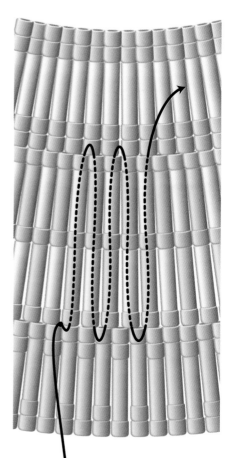

JOINING SUBSEQUENT LADDERS

The first two ladders are fairly easy to join because the needle always exits either at the inner or outer edge of the circle. To join the next ladders to the first two, you sew through the bead units of the new ladder and the ladder before it. As you exit the inner ladder, it gets a little tricky because the point of the needle will want to enter the outer edge of the adjoining ladder.

As you work around the circle, temporarily unpin a small section of both of the ladders you are working on and slide one or two fingers underneath, just enough to lift the inner ladder. Now you will have enough space for the needle to exit the inner edge. With your other hand, grasp the needle (with pliers, if necessary) to pull the thread through the bead unit. As you complete each section, replace the pins to secure the beadwork to the template.

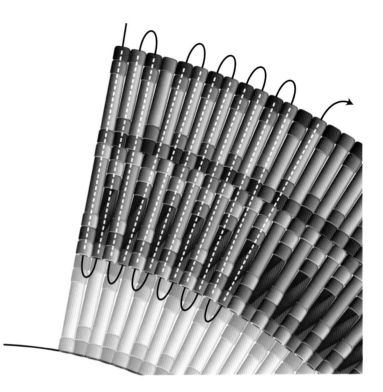

chapter 4
Decorative Elements

The ladders give beaded neckpieces their shape, but the additional decorative elements—and how you arrange them—is what gives the piece its unique style and visual interest. For example, the netting in Spike on page 79 is layered on a ladder to add density. A similar style of netting creates open space in Chartreuse on page 51, to lighten the dense design.

PLANNING THREAD PASSES

Any ladder unit that is joined to ladders before and after it will contain four strands of thread: one to string the individual units, one to build the ladder, one to join the ladder to the ladder that precedes it, and one to join it to the ladder that follows.

The most important thing is to make sure that no bead becomes so clogged with thread that the needle cannot pass through it. When you're adding decorative elements, try to make the most of each pass of thread. As you plan, consider how you can combine steps to make efficient use of the small space within each bead. Here are some guidelines for planning the thread passes in projects with decorative elements.

NETTING

Netting is a way to join two ladders, but it is also a versatile decorative element. It can be as simple as singular netted spokes or as elaborate as wide, dense nets with multiple connections. A netted spike is a singular piece of netting with no connections other than those from one row to the next.

There are two ways to create decorative netting. You can edge it with lacy picots, which you can then use to attach the subsequent ladder. Or you can work the netting back and forth between ladders to create a decorative space between them.

You can also add netting at the inner edge of the top ladder to create a small "collar." The netting will gently rise up the slope of the wearer's neck. Netting also makes a great base for fringe at the outermost edge of the neckpiece.

PICOTS

Picots are a simple way to decorate an otherwise plain edge. You can add them to any open ladder. Picots usually consist of one to three beads. Each picot is a separate element, so you can add one at a time wherever you'd like—maybe in place of a netted spike or a strand of fringe. Picots are easy to make and they're extremely versatile. They set up accessible beads that you can use to attach netting, a subsequent ladder, or any number of other elements.

Netting and Surface Embellishment
Meadow (page 65)

As you add netting to the inner edge of the first ladder, also add pressed-glass flowers between the first and second ladders.

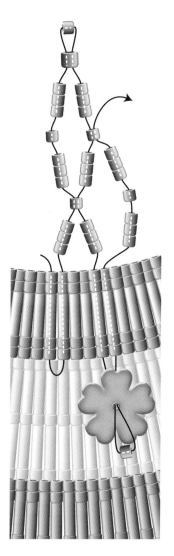

Netting and Picots
Chartreuse (page 51)

Add picots to the inner edge of the first ladder at the same time that you add netting to the outer edge of the same ladder.

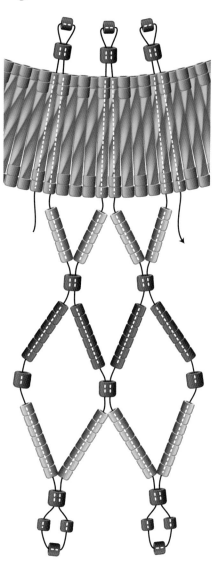

Joining Ladders and Picots
Gradient (page 87)

Add picots to the inner edge of the first ladder as you join the first and second ladders.

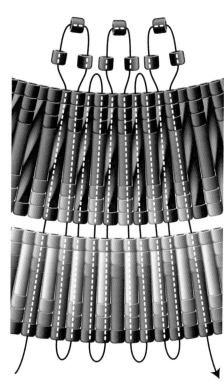

SURFACE EMBELLISHMENT

Surface embellishments provide easy ways to add extra dimension to your neckpiece. All you need is a small decorative element and a seed bead to hold it in place. You can add many types of embellishments to your beaded neckpiece—pressed glass, stone chips, or small crystal beads.

It's easiest to incorporate the embellishment into the neckpiece as you are adding other elements. For example, I added coral pieces to the surface of Ember on page 73 while making picots along the inner edge. I added the pressed-glass flowers in Meadow on page 65 while I was netting the inside edge and fringing the bottom one.

FRINGE

Fringe adds drama to a neckpiece. It also adds an appealing dynamic element, because the fringe moves as the wearer does. Fringe can vary in length, depending on the finished effect you want. It is also an excellent way to incorporate large decorative beads and other components into any neckpiece.

For example, a favorite bead or crystal strung on the center fringe strand makes a striking centerpiece. Intensely colored fringe beads will create strong contrast in a monochromatic piece. A branched fringe will add a touch of wild flair to the design. There are no rules with fringe (unlike the other elements in a beaded neckpiece), so use your imagination!

Layering and Picots
Spike (page 79)

Add a layer of netting over the third ladder as you make picots along the bottom edge of the fourth ladder.

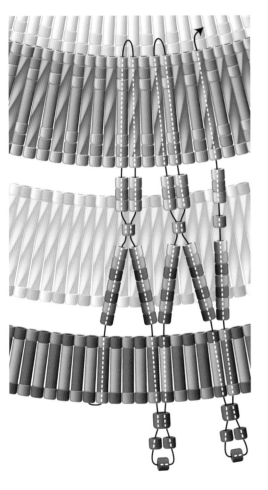

Picots and Surface Embellishment
Ember (page 73)

As you add picots to the inner edge of the first ladder, also add coral embellishments between the first and second ladders.

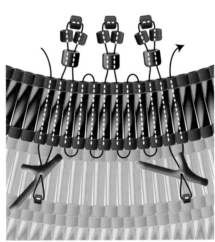

Fringe and Surface Embellishment
Trellis (page 103)

Add coral chips between the last two ladders as you add fringe to the outer edge of the neckpiece.

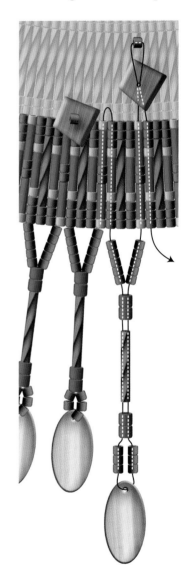

chapter 5
Finishing

When you have completed the neckpiece, remove it from the template. Now you need to affix a clasp to the ends so that you can wear it! You have some choices as to how to close the ladder ends. For lightweight neckpieces, you can add a bead and loop closure, as shown below.

For a heavier neckpiece, you need a stronger closure, such as a sturdy clasp attached to a pair of metal reducers.

ATTACHING THE FINDING

The sturdiest way to close your neckpiece is to fit the ends of the innermost ladder(s) with a strong finding. You need one that can accommodate a jump ring for the clasp you'll add later. Metal reducers, which are often used for stringing multiple strands of beads, are excellent choices.

The most common types of reducers have three holes on one side and one hole on the other. They are usually about 15 mm wide from end to end. Hold the multiple-hole side against the innermost ladder of the neckpiece. Most likely, the reducer and the ladder will be the same height, so you can attach the top edge of the ladder to the first hole and the bottom edge to the last hole.

If the reducer is too long, simply attach the bottom edge of the ladder to a different hole or, if it is long enough, allow it to span two ladders.

Begin a new thread. Choose a thread color that matches the neckpiece, because this thread will be visible. It's best to weave it through a ladder other than the one that will hold the reducer. Exit the inner edge of an end bead unit. Sew through the first hole of the reducer and then back through the same bead unit. Sew through the hole on the opposite end of the reducer. Repeat these steps several times, securely attaching the reducer to each end of the bead unit.

Weave the thread into your beadwork to finish. Before you do, you can weave a bead into each hole of the reducer to give it a more finished appearance.

Eventually, you will run out of room for the thread within the bead unit. Reinforce the reducer by carefully weaving back and forth between the threads that connect the ladder until you reach the next unit into which you can sew. Sew back and forth until the reducer is securely attached.

Repeat the entire process at the opposite end of the ladder, then weave the remaining thread ends into the neckpiece, as described on page 24.

ATTACHING THE CLASP

When you have finished the ends of your neckpiece, you can attach a clasp with one or more jump rings. Because these beaded neckpieces tend to be heavier than standard necklaces, be sure that the clasp is sturdy enough to hold a fair amount of weight. There are four types of clasps that work best: lobster-claw clasps, S hooks, toggles, and magnetic clasps.

Lobster-claw clasps include a lever that, when you pull it with your thumb, triggers a pin to open and close so that you can hook the jump ring on the opposite end of the neckpiece. With an S hook, you connect jump rings on either side of the neckpiece ends. Toggles have a small metal bar on one end that is inserted into a ring on the other end to close the neckpiece. Strong magnetic clasps firmly join the ends of the neckpiece and require little effort.

For extra security, you can also attach a safety chain to the closure by linking the jump ring on each end of the chain to the bottom holes of the metal reducers. The chain spans from one half of the reducer to the other. This way, if the clasp should open accidentally, the chain will hold the necklace in place until you can refasten it. Be sure the chain is long enough to allow the neck opening to fit over your head.

ATTACHING THE COUNTERWEIGHT

If your neckpiece is front-heavy—that is, if it has lots of beads, fringe, or other decorative elements that add weight to the front—you might want to add a counterweight at the back. Counterweights also add an elegant finish and a point of interest at the back of the piece. For example, because there is so much fringe on Eagle Feather, page 95, I added a beaded stone counterweight.

You can also add decorative metal coins or a metal fishing weight. Just link the element to one or both of the reducers or to the center of the safety chain, using jump rings or loops of beads or chain, as shown in the drawings at right.

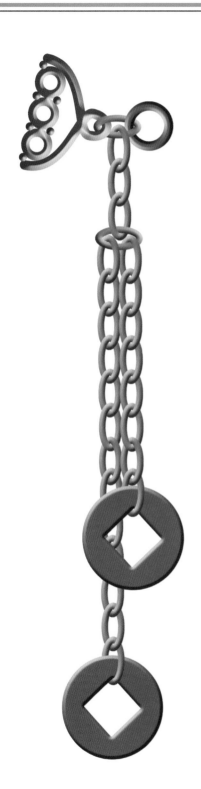

Projects

About the Projects

These ten projects are arranged in order of complexity, from the simplest to the most advanced. Before you begin the project you'd like to make, read through the instructions and, if necessary, review the discussion of the techniques presented in the early chapters.

FINDING YOUR SIZE

At the beginning of each project you will find a list of materials. Notice that there are three different bead amounts indicated for each component. The amounts you use depend on the diameter of the circle you've drawn on your template, which corresponds to the size of your neckpiece.

Check your measurements to find which size to follow:

size A: for a circle less than 13 cm in diameter
size B: for a circle from 13.1 to 16 cm in diameter
size C: for a circle from 16.1 to 19 cm in diameter

HELPFUL TIPS

Here are some guidelines to refer to as you make any of the projects in this book. They will also help you when you are making neckpieces that you design yourself.

- Sometimes, you may not be able to find the drop beads or perfectly match the colors of bugle and seed beads recommended for the projects. Don't worry. Just substitute beads with the colors and shapes that you like.

- Unless the directions say otherwise, pin every first ladder onto the template from clasp mark to clasp mark. Pin every subsequent ladder from one end of the previous row to the other end of that row.

- Avoid having extra thread ends by working with a double length of thread and placing a stopper bead half-way along the doubled length. When you have completed the first half of the netting, remove the stopper bead and work the second half of the netting with the long thread tail. To prevent tangles, coil the end and tape it underneath your work surface until you need it.

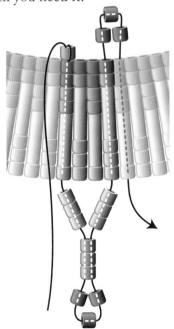

- At times, when joining a ladder to netting or picots, the center point of the net or picot will not align with the right bead unit. You can usually slightly readjust the ladder or the netting to correct the problem. If you can't, simply sew into the next unit, then reverse direction and sew backward to catch the point you missed. When the net or picot is in place, continue sewing in the original direction.

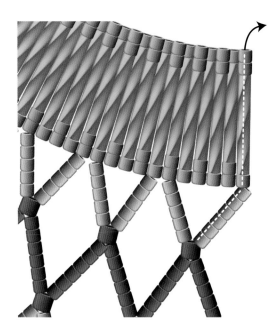

- Don't worry if your netting does not perfectly correspond with the number of bead units at either end of the ladder. When you reach the last unit, simply adjust the number of skipped beads between the top netted points so that the end of the last net joins with the last unit, as shown in the top drawing at right. Omit or add a bead or two if necessary, as shown in the bottom drawing at right.

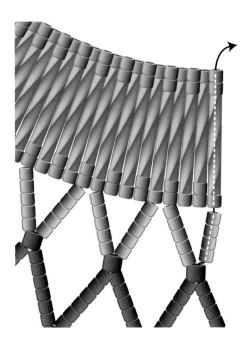

- When adding decorative elements, always begin in the center of the ladder. Working from this starting point will help you create a strong symmetrical design.

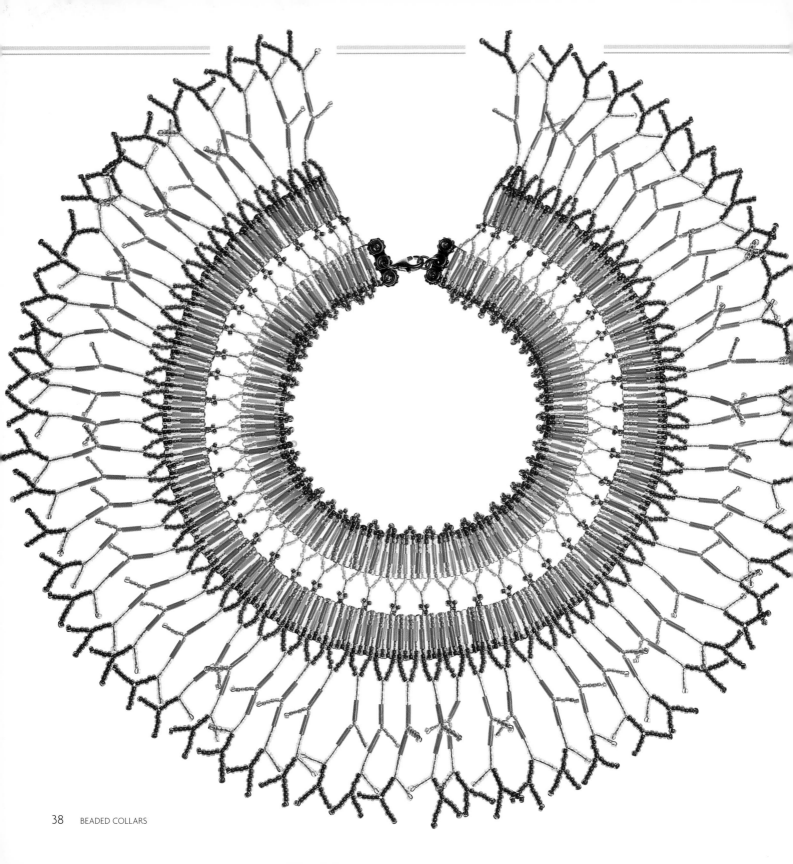

Urchin

This delicate collar combines branched fringe and open spaces for an airy feel.

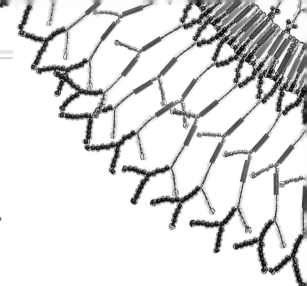

BEAD KEY

6mm untwisted white bugles
size A = 20 g; size B = 23 g;
size C = 27 g

11° white seeds
size A = 18 g; size B = 22 g;
size C = 25 g

11° light pink seeds
size A = 20 g; size B = 23 g;
size C = 27 g

11° dark pink seeds
size A = 29 g; size B = 34 g;
size C = 39 g

Step A: Ladder 1

Unit 1 (top to bottom)

• 11° dark pink seeds x 2
• 11° light pink seeds x 2
• 6mm untwisted white bugle x 1
• 11° white seed x 1

Unit 2 (bottom to top)

• 11° white seeds x 3
• 6mm untwisted white bugle x 1
• 11° light pink seed x 1
• 11° dark pink seed x 1

Build ladder 1 and pin it to the template.

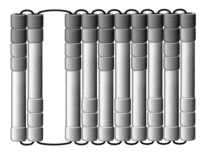

Step B: Netting and Inner Picot

Begin at the center of ladder 1 and work from left to right. Find the two units nearest to the halfway point. Count one unit outward on both sides for a total of four bead units. Sew through the first of the four units, exiting the outside of ladder 1.

Pick up:

• 11° white seeds x 3
• 11° light pink seeds x 3
• 11° dark pink seeds x 3

Sew back up through the three 11° light pink seeds, making sure not to split the thread. Pick up three 11° white seeds and sew through the last of the four bead units, skipping the two center units and exiting the inside of ladder 1. This is your first net.

Pick up three 11° dark pink seeds. Moving to the right, sew through the next unit, exiting the outside of ladder 1. This is your first picot.

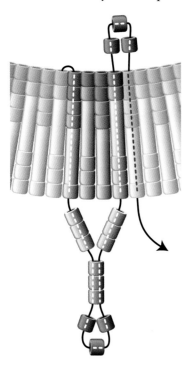

Repeat these steps to the end of the ladder. Remove the stopper bead from the tail and place a needle on the end. Add netting and picots to the remainder of the ladder. Pin all of the netted ends in place so that they are stretched taut and evenly distributed.

Step C: Ladder 2

Unit 1 (top to bottom)

- 11° white seed x 1
- 6mm untwisted white bugle x 1
- 11° light pink seeds x 2
- 11° dark pink seeds x 2

Unit 2 (bottom to top)

- 11° dark pink seed x 1
- 11° light pink seed x 1
- 6mm untwisted white bugle x 1
- 11° white seeds x 3

Ladder 2 will wrap around the outer points of the netting from the previous row. The first unit and the last unit will extend from the first to the last netted point.

Build ladder 2 and pin it to the template.

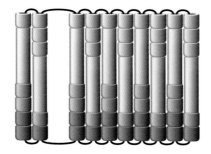

Sew through the first unit of ladder 2, exiting the inside edge, and then through the 11° dark pink seed at the bottom center of the first net. Sew through the next unit, exiting the outside edge. Weave in and out through the ladder until you reach the next netted point. Sew through this point. Continue to the end of the ladder, joining net points as you reach them.

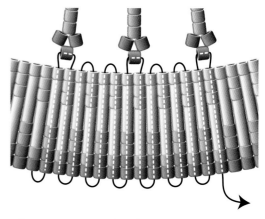

Step D: Branched Fringe

Begin at the center of ladder 2 and work from left to right. Find the unit nearest to the halfway point. Count two units outward on both sides for a total of five bead units. Sew through the first of the five units, exiting the outside of ladder 2.

Pick up:

- 11° dark pink seeds x 5
- 11° light pink seeds x 5
- 6mm untwisted white bugle bead x 1
- 11° white seeds x 2
- 6mm untwisted white bugle bead x 1
- 11° light pink seeds x 5
- 11° dark pink seeds x 11

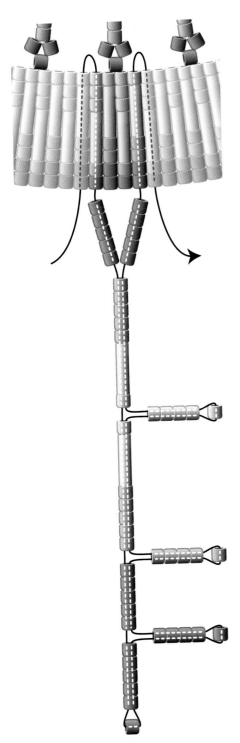

Skip the last bead and sew back through the next five beads. String five 11° dark pink seeds, skip the last bead, and sew through the next four beads to complete the first branch.

Sew through the next five 11° dark pink seeds. String five 11° light pink seeds, skip the last bead, and sew through the next four beads to complete the second branch.

Sew through the next seven beads, exiting the first of two 11° white seeds. String five 11° white seeds, skip the last bead, and sew through the next four beads to complete the last branch.

Sew through the next seven beads. Pick up five 11° dark pink seeds.

Enter the outside of ladder 2 through the unit that is three units away from the one that you last exited (you will have skipped two bead units).

Sew through the next unit, exiting the outside of ladder 2, and begin the next strand of branched fringe. Work to the end of the ladder. Repeat for the second half of the neckpiece.

Step E: Finishing

Add a closure to the open ends of the neckpiece. Weave in the thread ends. Attach a clasp. If necessary, refer to the finishing technique instructions on pages 30–32.

New Mexico

The bold colors and rhythmic patterns of this design evoke the landscape of the American Southwest.

BEAD KEY

6mm twisted dark red bugles
size A = 9 g; size B = 11 g;
size C = 12 g

6mm untwisted orange bugles
size A = 9 g; size B = 11 g;
size C = 12 g

6mm untwisted lavender bugles
size A = 9 g; size B = 10 g;
size C = 11 g

11° dark red seeds
size A = 9 g; size B = 10 g;
size C = 11 g

11° dusty rose seeds
size A = 33 g; size B = 38 g;
size C = 43 g

11° white seeds
size A = 13 g; size B = 15 g;
size C = 17 g

8° purple seeds
size A = 8 g; size B = 9 g;
size C = 10 g

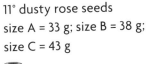

6mm x 8mm purple drops
(vertical hole)
size A = 13 beads; size B = 16 beads;
size C = 19 beads

Large rust-colored daggers
All sizes = 45 beads

Step A: Ladder 1

Unit 1 (top to bottom)

- 11° dusty rose seed x 1
- 6mm twisted dark red bugle x 1
- 11° dusty rose seed x 1
- 11° white seed x 1
- 11° dusty rose seed x 1

Unit 2 (bottom to top)

- 11° white seed x 1
- 6mm untwisted orange bugle x 1
- 11° white seed x 1
- 11° dusty rose seed x 1
- 11° white seed x 1

Build ladder 1 and pin it to the template.

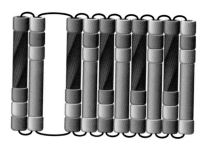

Step B: Top Netting

Begin at the center of ladder 1 and work from left to right. Find the bead unit nearest to the halfway point. Count two units outward on both sides for a total of five bead units. Sew through the first of the five units, exiting the inside of ladder 1.

Pick up seven 11° dusty rose seeds. Skip the last three beads and sew through the fourth bead, making sure not to split the thread.

Pick up three 11° dusty rose seeds and sew through the last of the five bead units, skipping the three center units and exiting the outside

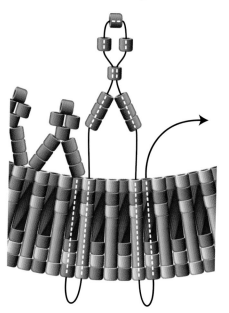

of ladder 1. Pull snug so that no thread is exposed. This is your first net.

Sew up through the next bead unit of ladder 1, exiting the inside edge. Continue to make nets to the end of the ladder. Repeat to build the remaining half of ladder 1.

Step C: Ladder 2

Unit 1 (top to bottom)

- 11° dark red seed x 1
- 11° dusty rose seed x 1
- 6mm untwisted lavender bugle x 1
- 11° dusty rose seed x 1

Unit 2 (bottom to top)

- 11° dark red seed x 1
- 11° dusty rose seed x 1
- 6mm untwisted lavender bugle x 1
- 11° dusty rose seed x 1

Build ladder 2 and pin it to the template.

Join ladder 1 and ladder 2.

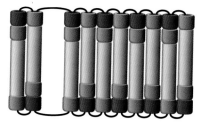

Step D: Picots, Drops, and Netting

Begin at the center of ladder 2 and work from left to right. Find the two bead units nearest to the halfway point. Count two units outward on both sides for a total of six bead units. Sew through the first of the six units, exiting the outside of ladder 2.

Pick up one 8° purple seed and one 11° dusty rose seed. Skip the 11° seed and sew up through the 8° seed and the next unit of ladder 2, making sure not to split the thread. This is your first picot. Sew back down through the next unit of ladder 2, exiting the outside edge.

Pick up one 8° purple seed, one purple drop, and one 11° dusty rose seed. Skip the last bead and sew up through the other two. Sew up through the next unit of ladder 2, exiting the inside edge, and then back out through the subsequent unit. Add one more picot to the other side of the drop.

Each net will occupy a total of five bead units.

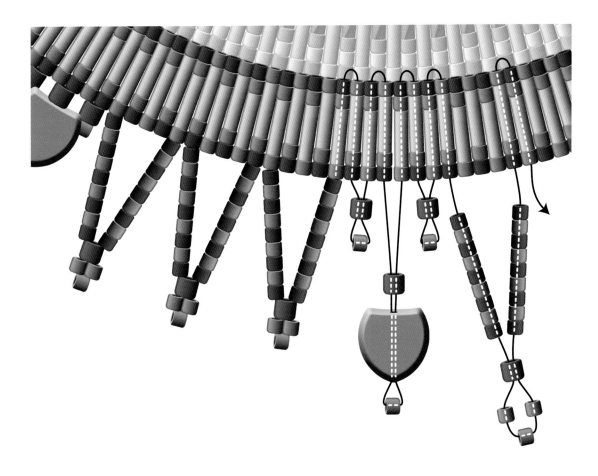

Pick up:

- 11° dark red seed x 1
- 11° dusty rose seed x 1
  (repeat four times)
- 11° dark red seed x 1
- 8° purple seed x 1
- 11° dusty rose seeds x 3

Skip the last three beads and sew up through the 8° purple seed, making sure not to split the thread.

Pick up:

- 11° dark red seed x 1
- 11° dusty rose seed x 1
  (repeat four times)
- 11° dark red seed x 1

Sew through the last of the five bead units, skipping the three center units and exiting the inside of ladder 2. Pull snug so that no thread is exposed. This is your first net.

Sew through the next bead unit of ladder 2, exiting the outside edge. Make two more net segments.

Continue this pattern, making a picot, a drop, a picot, and then three net segments to the end of the ladder. Be sure to end the ladder with a net segment, even if it means ending with more than three net segments. Repeat for the remaining half of ladder 2, beginning with three net segments.

Pin all of the netted ends in place so that they are stretched taut and evenly distributed.

Step E: Ladder 3

Ladder 3 will wrap around the outer points of the netting from the previous row. The first unit and the last unit will extend from the first to the last netted point.

Unit 1 (top to bottom)

- 11° dusty rose seed x 1
- 11° white seed x 1
- 11° dusty rose seed x 1
- 6mm twisted dark red bugle x 1
- 11° dusty rose seed x 1

Unit 2 (bottom to top)

- 11° white seed x 1
- 11° dusty rose seed x 1
- 11° white seed x 1
- 6mm untwisted orange bugle x 1
- 11° white seed x 1

Build ladder 3 and pin it to the template.

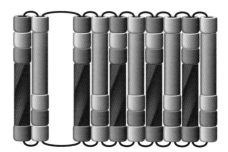

Sew through the first unit of ladder 3, exiting the inside edge, and then through the 11° dusty rose seed at the bottom center of the first net. Sew through the next unit, exiting the outside edge. Weave in and out through the ladder until you reach the next netted point. Sew through this point. Continue to the end of the ladder, joining net points as you reach them.

The fringe for this neckpiece contains forty-five strands and occupies ninety bead units. The remainder of the bottom edge of ladder 3 is lined with picots. Find the two bead units nearest to the halfway point. Sew through the first of the two bead units, exiting the outside edge.

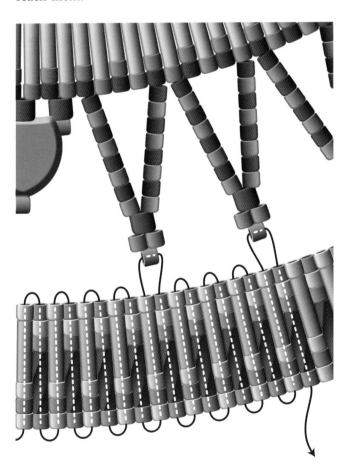

Step F: Long Fringe

Pick up:

- 11° dusty rose seed x 1
- 11° white seed x 1
  (repeat five more times)
- 11° dusty rose seed x 1
- 8° purple seed x 1
- 6mm untwisted lavender bugle x 1
- 8° purple seed x 1
- 11° dark red seed x 1
- 11° dusty rose seed x 1
- 11° dark red seed x 1
  (repeat four more times)
- Large rust-colored dagger x 1
- 11° dark red seed x 1
- 11° dusty rose seed x 1
- 11° dark red seed x 1
- 11° dusty rose seed x 1
- 11° dark red seed x 1

Skip five seed beads on either side of the dagger and sew up through the remainder of the strand. Then sew through the second of the two center units, exiting the inside of ladder 3. Turn and sew through the subsequent bead unit.

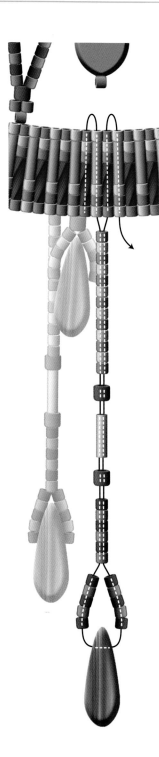

Step G: Short Dagger Loop

Pick up:

- 8° purple seed x 1
- 11° dusty rose seed x 1
- 11° white seed x 1
- 11° dusty rose seed x 1
- 11° white seed x 1
- 11° dusty rose seed x 1
- Large rust dagger x 1
- 11° dusty rose seed x 1
- 11° white seed x 1
- 11° dusty rose seed x 1
- 11° white seed x 1
- 11° dusty rose seed x 1

Sew up through the 8° purple seed and then through the next bead unit, exiting the inside of ladder 3. Turn and sew through the subsequent bead unit.

Repeat this process, alternating between long fringe strands and short dagger loops to the ⅜ mark on your template.

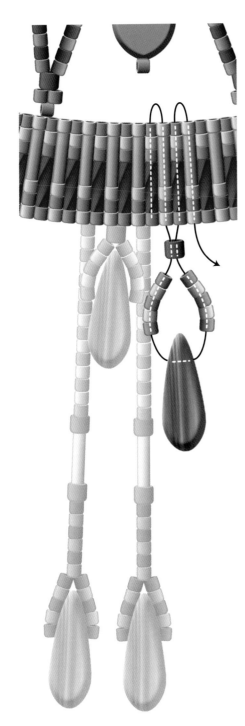

Step H: Picots

Pick up one 8° purple seed and three 11° dusty rose seeds. Skip the rose seeds and sew through the purple seed and then up through the next bead unit. This is your first picot. Turn and exit the outside edge of ladder one.

Continue to add a picot between every two bead units, working to the end of the ladder. Repeat this entire process to complete the remaining half of ladder 3.

Step I: Finishing

Add a closure to the open ends of the neckpiece. Weave in the thread ends. Attach a clasp. If necessary, refer to the finishing technique instructions on pages 30–32.

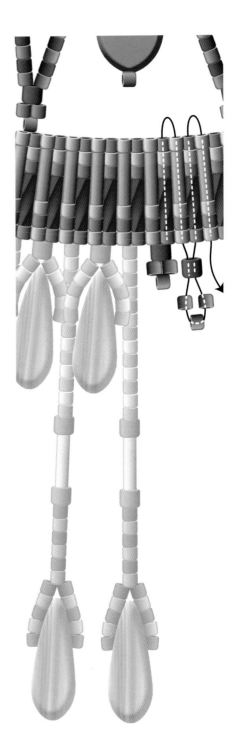

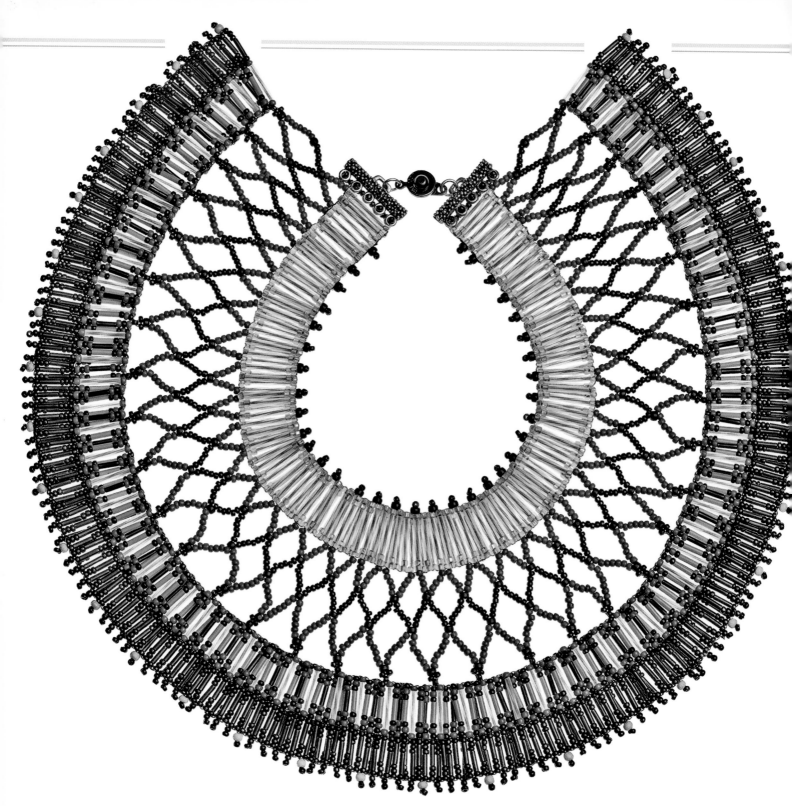

Chartreuse

This bold design combines techniques to create broad netting and picoted fringe.

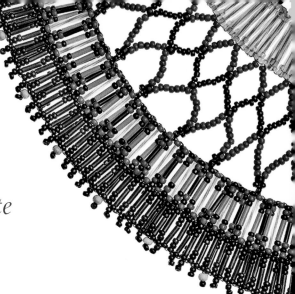

BEAD KEY

12mm twisted chartreuse bugles
size A = 20 g; size B = 23 g;
size C = 27 g

6mm untwisted purple bugles
size A = 16 g; size B = 17 g;
size C = 19 g

6mm untwisted lavender bugles
size A = 6 g; size B = 7 g;
size C = 7 g

11° purple seeds
size A = 36 g; size B = 41 g;
size C = 46 g

11° lavender seeds
size A = 19 g; size B = 23 g;
size C = 26 g

11° chartreuse seeds
size A = 7 g; size B = 8 g;
size C = 9 g

8° purple seeds
size A = 5 g; size B = 6 g;
size C = 7 g

8° chartreuse seeds
size A = 2 g; size B = 2 g;
size C = 2 g

Step A: Ladder 1

Unit 1 (top to bottom)
- 11° chartreuse seeds x 2
- 12mm twisted chartreuse bugle x 1
- 11° chartreuse seed x 1

Unit 2 (bottom to top)
- 11° chartreuse seeds x 2
- 12mm twisted chartreuse bugle x 1
- 11° chartreuse seed x 1

Build ladder 1 and pin it to the template.

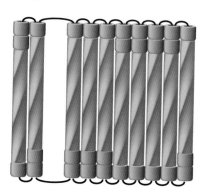

Step B: Picots and Netting

Begin at the center of ladder 1 and work from left to right. Find the two bead units nearest to the half-way point. Count two units outward on both sides for a total of six bead units. Sew through the first unit, exiting the inside of ladder 1.

Pick up one 8° purple seed and one 11° purple seed. Skip the last seed and sew through the 8° seed and then through the next bead unit, exiting the outside edge of ladder 1. This is your first picot.

Pick up:

- 11° lavender seed x 5
- 8° purple seed x 1
- 11° purple seeds x 6
- 8° purple seed x 1
- 11° lavender seeds x 7
- 8° purple seed x 1
- 11° purple seeds x 3

Skip the last three beads and sew through the next 8° seed. Pick up seven 11° lavender seeds, one 8° seed, and six purple seeds, then sew through the first 8° added for the netting. Pick up five 11° lavender seeds, skip three bead units, and sew through the last of the bead units, exiting the inside edge of ladder 1. This is your first net.

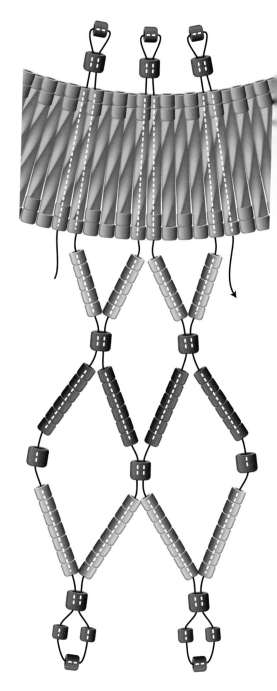

Make another picot and sew through the next bead unit, exiting the outside of ladder 1. Begin the next segment.

Pick up:
• 11° lavender seeds x 5
• 8° purple seed x 1
• 11° purple seeds x 6

Sew through the first open 8° purple seed. Complete this net segment as you did the previous one. Continue to add picots and netting to the end of the ladder. Complete the remaining half of the ladder in the same manner.

Step C: Ladder 2

Ladder 2 will wrap around the outer points of the netting from the previous row. The first unit and the last unit will extend from the first to the last netted point.

Unit 1 (top to bottom)
• 11° lavender seed x 1
• 12mm twisted chartreuse bugle x 1
• 11° lavender seed x 1

Unit 2 (bottom to top)
• 11° purple seed x 1
• 11° lavender seed x 1
• 11° purple seed x 1
• 6mm untwisted lavender bugle x 1
• 11° purple seed x 1
• 11° lavender seed x 1
• 11° purple seed x 1

Unit 3 (top to bottom)
• 11° lavender seed x 1
• 11° purple seed x 1
• 11° lavender seed x 1
• 6mm untwisted purple bugle x 1
• 11° lavender seed x 1
• 11° purple seed x 1
• 11° lavender seed x 1

Unit 4 (bottom to top)
• 11° purple seed x 1
• 11° lavender seed x 1
• 11° purple seed x 1
• 6mm untwisted lavender bugle x 1
• 11° purple seed x 1
• 11° lavender seed x 1
• 11° purple seed x 1

Build ladder 2 and pin it to the template.

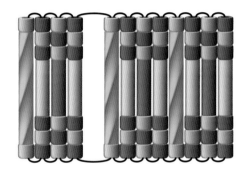

Sew through the first unit of ladder 2, exiting the inside edge, and then through the 11° purple seed at the bottom center of the first net. Sew through the next unit, exiting the outside edge. Weave in and out through the ladder until you reach the next netted point. Sew through this point. Continue to the end of the ladder, joining net points as you reach them.

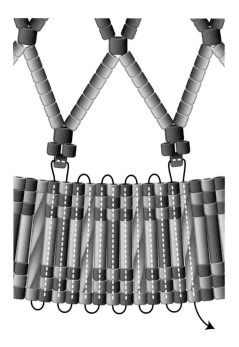

Step D: Ladder 3

Unit 1 (top to bottom)

• 11° purple seed x 1
• 6mm untwisted purple bugle x 1
• 11° purple seeds x 3

Unit 2 (bottom to top)

• 11° purple seed x 1
• 6mm untwisted purple bugle x 1
• 11° purple seeds x 3

Build ladder 3 and pin it to the template. Join ladder 2 and ladder 3.

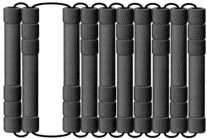

Step E: Short Fringe and Picots

Begin at the center of ladder 3 and work from left to right. Find the two bead units nearest to the halfway point. Sew through the first of the two units, exiting the outside of ladder 3.

Pick up one 8° chartreuse seed and one 11° purple seed. Skip the last seed and sew through the 8° seed and then through the next bead unit, exiting the inside edge of ladder 3. This is your first picot.

Turn and sew through the next bead unit to exit the outside of ladder 3. Pick up three 11° purple seeds. Skip the last seed and sew up through the other two and then through the next bead unit, exiting the inside of ladder 3. Repeat this step three more times until you have four short fringe strands.

Make another picot.

Continue to make four short fringe strands for every picot as you work to the end of the ladder. Repeat the steps to complete the remaining half of the ladder.

Step F: Finishing

Add a closure to the open ends of the neckpiece. Weave in the thread ends. Attach a clasp. If necessary, refer to the finishing technique instructions on pages 30–32.

Drab

Subtle color changes give this neckpiece an air of simple elegance.

BEAD KEY

12mm twisted brown metallic bugles
size A = 21 g; size B = 24 g;
size C = 28 g

6mm untwisted dark green metallic bugles
size A = 22 g; size B = 26 g;
size C = 29 g

11° dark green luster seeds
size A = 72 g; size B = 83 g;
size C = 94 g

8° brown matte metallic seeds
size A = 3 g; size B = 4 g;
size C = 4 g

6mm assorted color pearls
size A = 17 pearls; size B = 24 pearls;
size C = 28 pearls

Step A: Ladder 1

Unit 1 (top to bottom)

- 11° dark green luster seed x 1
- 12mm twisted brown metallic bugle x 1
- 11° dark green luster seed x 1

Unit 2 (bottom to top)

- 11° dark green luster seeds x 3
- 6mm untwisted dark green metallic bugle x 1
- 11° dark green luster seeds x 3

Build ladder 1 and pin it to the template.

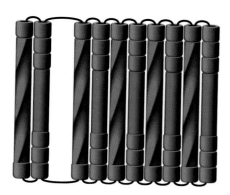

Step B: Ladder 2 and Netting

In this neckpiece, ladder 2 does *not* wrap around ladder 1. Instead, measure 1.5 cm from the outside edge of ladder 1 and mark it on the halfway line. Make a new circle by setting your compass from the center of the template to the 1.5 cm mark on the halfway marker line. You'll use this circle as a guide when pinning ladder 2 to the template. The netting will span the distance between the two ladders.

Unit 1 (top to bottom)

- 11° dark green luster seed x 1
- 12mm twisted brown metallic bugle x 1
- 11° dark green luster seed x 1

Unit 2 (bottom to top)

- 11° dark green luster seeds x 3
- 6mm untwisted dark green metallic bugle x 1
- 11° dark green luster seeds x 3

Build ladder 2 and pin it to the template.

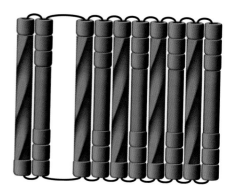

Begin at the center of ladder 1 and work from left to right. Find the two units nearest to the halfway point. Sew through the unit first of the two units, exiting the outside of ladder 1.

Pick up:

- 11° dark green luster seed x 1
- 8° brown matte metallic seed x 1
- 6mm pearl x 1
- 8° brown matte metallic seed x 1
- 11° dark green luster seed x 1

Make a ray by extending a length of thread from the center point of the template and between the two center units of ladder 1 to the corresponding pair of bead units for ladder 2. For the first net, the ray will be on the vertical centerline of the template. Sew through the first unit, exiting the outside of ladder 2. Sew through the next unit, exiting the inside of the ladder.

Pick up one 11° dark green luster seed. Skip the first 11° bead of the net and sew through the next three beads. Pick up one 11° dark green luster seed and sew through the next bead unit of ladder 1. This is your first net.

Sew down and then up through the next two bead units. Pick up three

11° dark green luster seeds and sew down through the next bead unit. This is your first picot.

Sew up and then down through the next two bead units. Pick up three 11° dark green luster seeds and sew up through the next bead unit to make a picot at the outside edge of ladder 1.

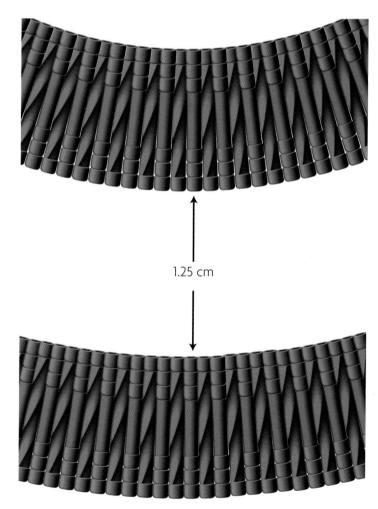

1.25 cm

Sew down and then up through the next two bead units. Pick up three 11° dark green luster seeds and sew up through the next bead unit to make a second picot at the inside edge of ladder 1.

Sew up and then down through the next two bead units and begin a new net. Continue to the end of the ladder.

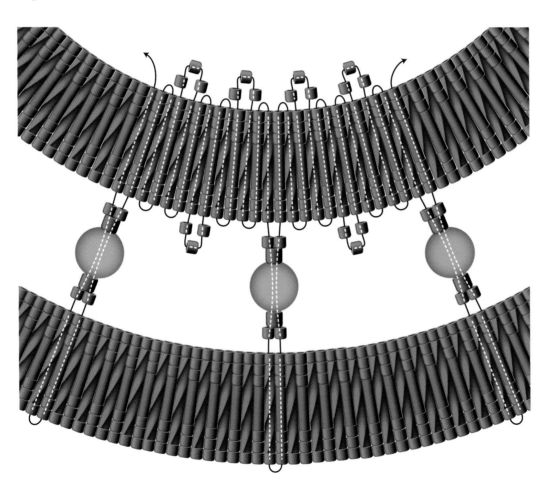

Ideally, both halves of ladder 1 will end with a net, which will ensure that ladder 2 is supported. If not, continue until you have three units remaining. Exit either the outside edge of ladder 1 or the inside of ladder 2, depending on the location of the last picot or net you made. Pick up a strand (usually 9 to 10 beads) of 11° dark green luster seeds. Sew through the corresponding bead unit so that the strand bridges the two ladders. Sew through the next unit and repeat this process two more times.

Step C: Ladder 3 and Picots

Unit 1 (top to bottom)

- 11° dark green luster seeds x 2
- 6mm untwisted dark green metallic bugle x 1
- 11° dark green luster seed x 1

Unit 2 (bottom to top)

- 11° dark green luster seeds x 2
- 6mm untwisted dark green metallic bugle x 1
- 11° dark green luster seed x 1

Build ladder 3 and pin it to the template.

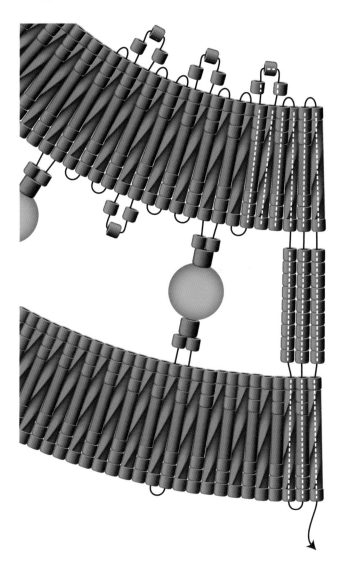

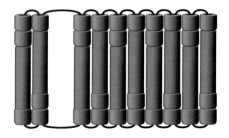

Join ladder 2 and ladder 3. Each time you exit the inside edge of ladder 2 at the midpoint between two nets, pick up three 11° dark green luster seeds to make a picot.

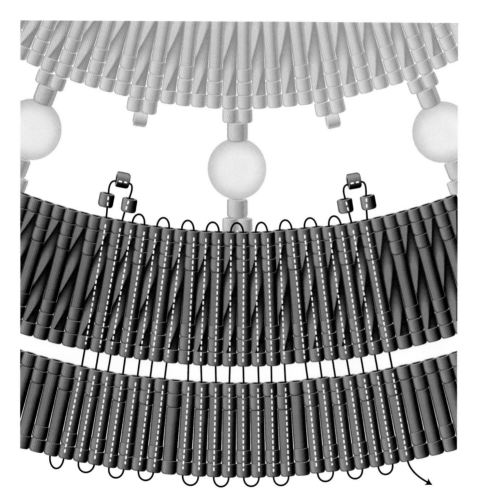

Step D: Fringe

Begin at the center of ladder 3 and work from left to right. Find the two bead units nearest to the halfway point. Sew through the first of the two units, exiting the outside of ladder 3.

Pick up:

- 8° brown matte metallic seed x 1
- 11° dark green luster seeds x 5
- 12mm twisted brown metallic bugle x 1
- 11° dark green luster seeds x 5
- 6mm untwisted dark green metallic bugle x 1
- 11° dark green luster seeds x 50
- 6mm untwisted dark green metallic bugle x 1
- 11° dark green luster seeds x 5
- 12mm twisted brown metallic bugle x 1
- 11° dark green luster seeds x 5

Sew back up through the 8° seed and the second center bead unit, forming a loop with the rest of the strand. Turn and sew through the next unit, exiting the outside of ladder 3.

To make the next fringe loop, pick up the same bead sequence as you did for the previous—but this time pick up forty-nine 11° dark green luster seeds instead of fifty.

Continue to make fringe loops, reducing the large group of beads by one bead each time, until you are working with twenty-five beads. Making no further reductions, continue making fringe loops until you reach the ⅜ line of your template.

Repeat this process to complete the remaining half of the bottom fringe.

Step E: Finishing

Add a closure to the open ends of the neckpiece. Weave in the thread ends. Attach a clasp. If necessary, refer to the finishing technique instructions on pages 30–32.

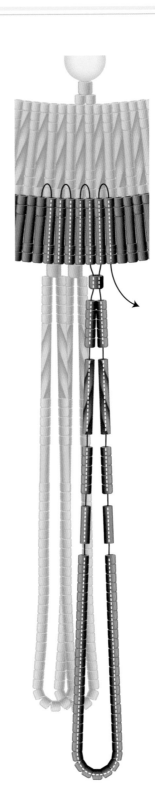

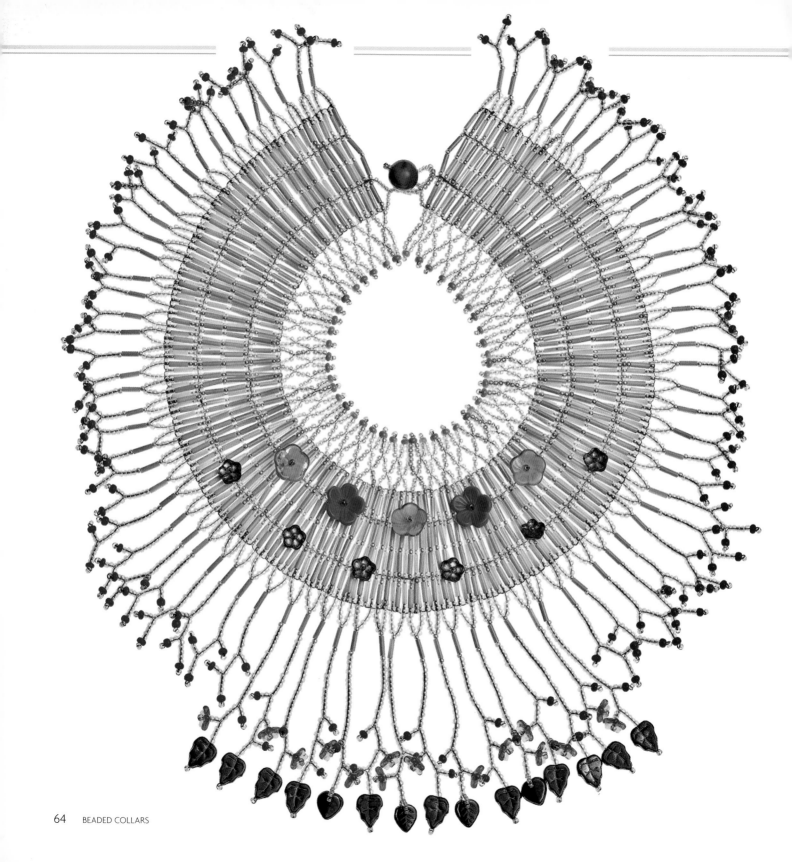

Meadow

Meadow combines brightly colored ladders and pressed-glass flowers to create the look and feel of springtime.

BEAD KEY

6mm untwisted cream bugles
size A = 8 g; size B = 9 g;
size C = 11 g

6mm untwisted yellow bugles
size A = 20 g; size B = 23 g;
size C = 26 g

11° pale yellow seeds
size A = 30 g; size B = 36 g;
size C = 42 g

11° pale green seeds
size A = 33 g; size B = 37 g;
size C = 42 g

8° yellow seeds
size A = 2 g; size B = 2 g;
size C = 3 g

8° pale blue seeds
size A = 8 g; size B = 9 g;
size C = 10 g

Small green pressed-glass flowers (6)

Small yellow pressed-glass flowers (15)

Large yellow pressed-glass flowers (3)

Large blue pressed-glass flowers (2)

Pressed-glass green leaves, with
vertical hole (15)

Step A: Ladder 1

Unit 1 (top to bottom)

- 11° pale yellow seeds x 2
- 6mm untwisted cream bugle x 1
- 11° pale yellow seed x 1

Unit 2 (bottom to top)

- 11° pale yellow seeds x 2
- 6mm untwisted cream bugle x 1
- 11° pale yellow seed x 1

Build ladder 1 and pin it to the template.

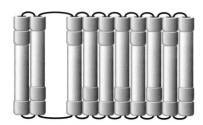

Step B: Ladder 2

Unit 1 (top to bottom)

- 11° pale yellow seed x 1
- 6mm untwisted yellow bugle x 1
- 11° pale yellow seed x 1
- 6mm untwisted cream bugle x 1
- 11° pale yellow seed x 1

Unit 2 (bottom to top)

- 11° pale yellow seed x 1
- 6mm untwisted yellow bugle x 1
- 11° pale yellow seed x 1
- 6mm untwisted cream bugle x 1
- 11° pale yellow seed x 1

Build ladder 2 and pin it to the template. Join ladder 1 and ladder 2.

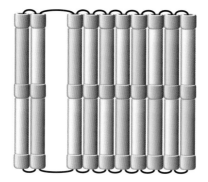

Step C: Ladder 3

Unit 1 (top to bottom)

- 11° pale yellow seed x 1
- 6mm untwisted yellow bugle x 1
- 11° pale green seeds x 2

Unit 2 (bottom to top)

- 11° pale green seed x 1
- 6mm untwisted yellow bugle x 1
- 11° pale yellow seeds x 2

Build ladder 3 and pin it to the template. Join ladder 2 and ladder 3.

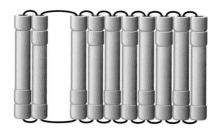

Step D: Top Netting and Surface Embellishment

Arrange the pressed glass flowers on the completed ladders in two rows: one row between ladders 1 and 2; the other between ladders 2 and 3. Very carefully pin each large yellow, large blue, and small green pressed-glass flower between the ladders, following the layout diagram on page 67 (or create your own design).

Begin the netting at the center of ladder 1 and work from left to right. Find the two bead units nearest to the halfway point. Sew through the second of the two units, exiting the inside of ladder 1.

Pick up:

- 11° pale yellow seeds x 3
- 11° pale green seed x 1
- 11° pale yellow seeds x 3
- 11° pale green seed x 1
- 11° pale yellow seeds x 3
- 8° yellow seed x 1
- 11° pale yellow seed x 1

Skip the last bead and sew through the 8° yellow seed.

Pick up:

- 11° pale yellow seeds x 3
- 11° pale green seed x 1
- 11° pale yellow seeds x 3

Skip the next seven beads and sew through the corresponding 11° pale green seed. String three 11° pale yellow seeds, skip two bead units from where you began, and sew through the next bead unit, exiting the outside of ladder 1. You may have to temporarily remove one or more pressed-glass flowers to perform this step. Sew back up through the next unit to continue the netting.

Whenever you reach a pressed-glass flower between the first and second ladders, sew through the back of the flower and pick up one 11° pale green seed. Sew back through the flower and then through the next bead unit, exiting the inside of ladder 1.

Pick up:

• 11° pale yellow seeds x 3
• 11° pale green seed x 1
• 11° pale yellow seeds x 3

Skip the first seven beads of the previous net segment and sew through the corresponding 11° pale green seed. Complete this net segment as you did the previous segment.

Continue to the end of ladder, netting the inside edge of ladder 1 and attaching pressed-glass flowers where necessary. Repeat this process to complete the netting on the remaining half of the ladder.

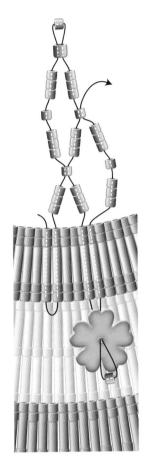

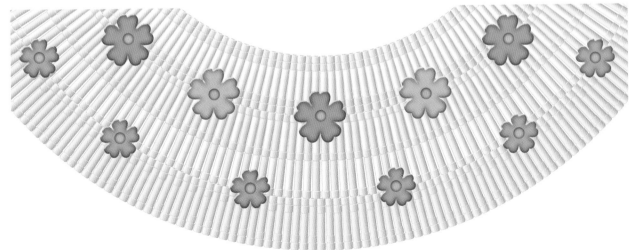

Step E: Fringe and Surface Embellishment

As you add strands of fringe to the outside edge of ladder 3, attach the remaining pressed-glass flowers to the neckpiece, as you did for the netting.

Begin the fringe at the center of ladder 3 and work from left to right. Find the bead unit nearest to the halfway point and count outward by one unit on each side for a total of three units. Sew through the first of the three units, exiting the outside of ladder 3.

The center section alternates between a three-branch fringe strand and a two-branch fringe strand.

Three-Branch Fringe Strand

Pick up:

- 11° pale green seeds x 5
- 11° pale yellow seed x 1
- 6mm untwisted yellow bugle x 1
- 11° pale yellow seed x 1
- 11° pale green seeds x 30
- pressed-glass green leaf x 1
- 11° pale green seed x 1

Skip the last seed and sew back through the leaf bead and the next five seed beads.

Pick up:

- 11° pale green seeds x 2
- 8° pale blue seed x 1
- 11° pale green seed x 1

Skip the last bead and sew through the remaining three to complete the first branch.
Sew through the next five 11° pale green seeds.

Pick up:

- 11° pale green seeds x 2
- small yellow pressed-glass flower x 1
- 11° pale green seed x 1

Skip the last bead and sew through the remaining three to complete the second branch.
Sew through the next five 11° pale green seeds.

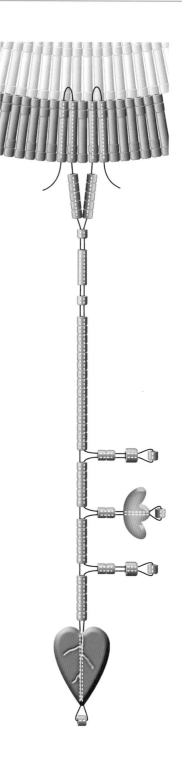

Pick up:

- 11° pale green seeds x 2
- 8° pale blue seed x 1
- 11° pale green seed x 1

Skip the last bead and sew through the remaining three to complete the third branch.

Sew through the next eighteen beads, stopping before the last five 11° pale green seeds. Pick up five 11° pale green seeds and sew through the last of the three bead units, exiting the inside of ladder 3. Attach a pressed-glass flower if necessary and sew through the next unit, exiting the outside edge of ladder 3.

Two-Branch Fringe Strand

Pick up:

- 11° pale green seeds x 5
- 11° pale yellow seed x 1
- 6mm untwisted yellow bugle x 1
- 11° pale yellow seed x 1
- 11° pale green seeds x 30
- pressed-glass green leaf x 1
- 11° pale green seed x 1

Skip the last seed and sew back through the leaf bead and the next five seed beads.

Pick up:

- 11° pale green seeds x 2
- small yellow pressed-glass flower x 1
- 11° pale green seed x 1

Skip the last bead and sew through the remaining three to complete the first branch. Sew through the next five 11° pale green seeds.

Pick up:

- 11° pale green seeds x 2
- 8° pale blue seed x 1
- 11° pale green seed x 1

Skip the last bead and sew through the remaining three to complete the second branch.
Sew through the next twenty-three beads, stopping before the last five 11° pale green seeds. Pick up five 11° pale green seeds and sew through the last of the three bead units, exiting on the inside of ladder 3. Attach a pressed-glass flower if necessary and sew through the next unit, exiting the outside edge of ladder 3.

Alternate between three- and two-branch fringe strands to make a total of eight strands. Next, you'll begin two levels of short branched fringe.

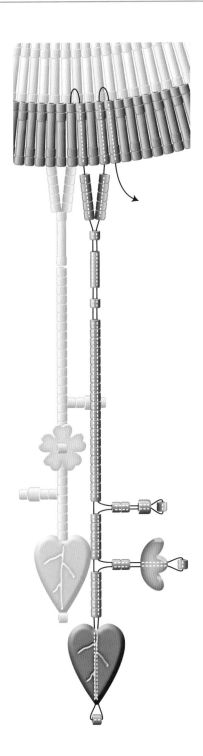

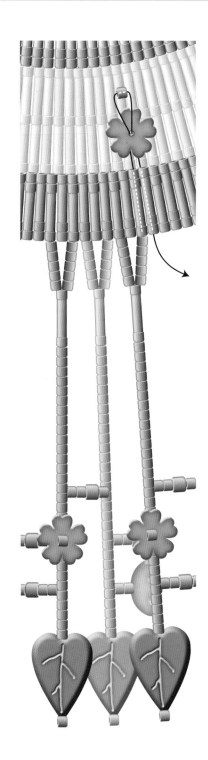

First Level (repeat eight times)

Pick up:

- 11° pale green seeds x 5
- 11° pale yellow seed x 1
- 6mm untwisted yellow bugle x 1
- 11° pale yellow seed x 1
- 11° pale green seeds x 20
- 8° pale blue seed x 1
- 11° pale green seed x 1

Skip the last seed and sew back through the 8° pale blue seed and the next five seed beads.

Pick up:

- 11° pale green seeds x 2
- 8° pale blue seed x 1
- 11° pale green seed x 1

Skip the last bead and sew through the remaining three to complete the first branch.

Sew through the next five 11° pale green seeds.

Pick up:

- 11° pale green seeds x 2
- 8° pale blue seed x 1
- 11° pale green seed x 1

Skip the last bead and sew through the remaining three to complete the second branch.

Sew through the next thirteen beads, stopping before the last five 11° pale green seeds. Pick up five 11° pale green seeds and sew through the last of the three bead units, exiting the inside of ladder 3. Attach a pressed-glass flower if necessary and sew through the next unit, exiting the outside edge of ladder 3.

Second Level (repeat to the end of the ladder)

Pick up:

• 11° pale green seeds x 5
• 11° pale yellow seed x 1
• 6mm untwisted yellow bugle x 1
• 11° pale yellow seed x 1
• 11° pale green seeds x 10
• 8° pale blue seed x 1
• 11° pale green seed x 1

Skip the last seed and sew back through the 8° pale blue seed and the next five seed beads.

Pick up:

• 11° pale green seeds x 2
• 8° pale blue seed x 1
• 11° pale green seed x 1

Skip the last bead and sew through the remaining three to complete the second branch.

Sew through the next eight beads, stopping before the last five 11° pale green seeds. Pick up five 11° pale green seeds and sew through the last of the three bead units, exiting the inside of ladder 3. Attach a pressed-glass flower if necessary and sew through the next unit, exiting the outside edge of ladder 3.

Repeat these steps to complete the remaining half of the ladder.

Step F: Finishing

Add a closure to the open ends of the neckpiece. Weave in the thread ends. Attach a clasp. If necessary, refer to the finishing technique instructions on pages 30–32.

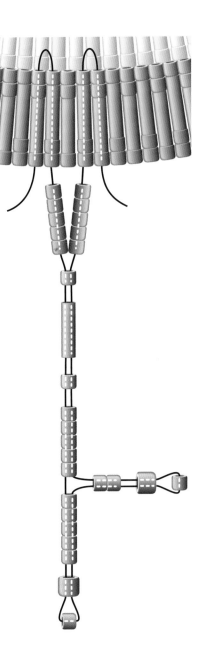

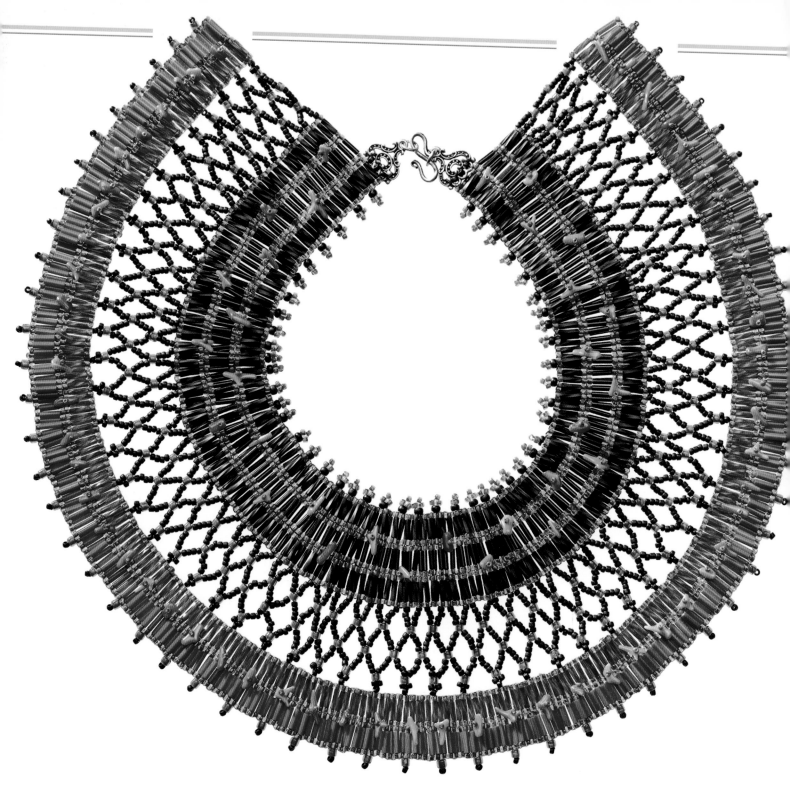

Ember

This fiery neckpiece has strong contrasting colors and tightly woven netting.

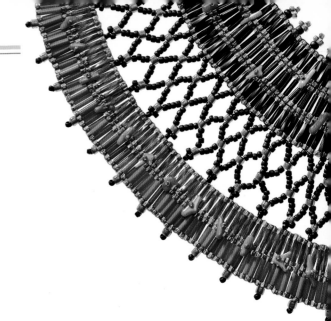

BEAD KEY

6mm twisted black matte bugles
size A = 16 g; size B = 19 g;
size C = 22 g

6mm untwisted black bugles
size A = 8 g; size B = 9 g;
size C = 10 g

6mm twisted red bugles
size A = 13 g; size B = 14 g;
size C = 16 g

6mm untwisted red bugles
size A = 13 g; size B = 14 g;
size C = 16 g

11° black seeds
size A = 19 g; size B = 22 g;
size C = 25 g

11° red seeds
size A = 3 g; size B = 3 g; size C = 4 g

8° black seeds
size A = 2 g; size B = 2 g; size C = 3 g

8° red seeds
size A = 2 g; size B = 3 g;
size C = 3 g

Small coral pieces
size A = 87 beads; size B = 123
beads; size C = 137 beads

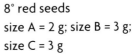

Step A: Ladder 1

All Units

- 11° red seed x 1
- 6mm twisted black matte bugle x 1
- 11° red seed x 1

Build ladder 1 and pin it to the template.

Step B: Ladder 2

All Units

- 11° red seed x 1
- 6mm untwisted black bugle x 1
- 11° red seed x 1

Build ladder 2 and pin it to the template. Join ladder 1 and ladder 2.

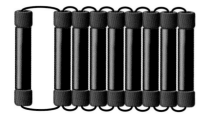

Step C: Ladder 3

All Units

- 11° red seed x 1
- 6mm twisted black matte bugle x 1
- 11° red seed x 1

Build ladder 3 and pin it to the template. Join ladder 2 and ladder 3.

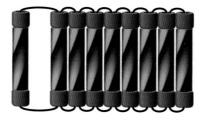

Step D: Top Picots and Surface Embellishment

Begin at the center of ladder 1 and work from left to right. Find the two bead units nearest to the halfway point. Sew through the first of the two units, exiting the inside of ladder 1.

Pick up one 8° black seed and three 11° red seeds. Skip the red seeds and sew through the black one and then through the second bead unit of the two-unit group, exiting the outside of ladder 1. Weave up, down, and up through the next three bead units and make a second picot.

When you have exited the outside edge of ladder 1, pick up one coral piece and one 11° red seed. Sew back through the coral piece and up through the next bead unit. Weave down and then up through the next two bead units and make another picot.

Continue in this manner, attaching a coral piece after every third picot, until you reach the end of the ladder. Repeat to complete the remaining half of ladder 1.

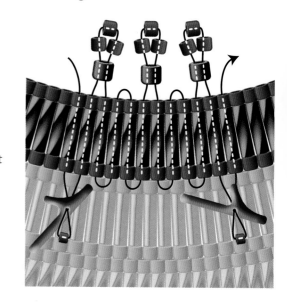

Step E: Netting and Surface Embellishment

Begin at the center of ladder 3 and work from left to right. Find the two bead units nearest the halfway point and count outward by one unit on each side for a total of four bead units. Sew through the first of the two units, exiting the outside of ladder 3.

Pick up:

- 11° black seeds x 4
- 8° red seed x 1
- 11° black seeds x 4
- 8° red seed x 1
- 11° black seeds x 4
- 8° red seed x 1
- 11° black seeds x 3

Skip the last three beads and sew through the 8° red seed.

Pick up:

- 11° black seeds x 4
- 8° red seed x 1
- 11° black seeds x 4

Skip the next nine beads and sew through the top 8° red seed. String four 11° black seeds and sew through the last bead unit in the four-unit group. Pick up one coral piece and one 11° red seed. Sew back through the coral piece and down through the next bead unit, exiting the outside of ladder 3. Now begin the next net segment.

Pick up:

- 11° black seeds x 4
- 8° red seed x 1
- 11° black seeds x 4

Sew through the middle 8° red seed. Complete this net segment as you did the first.

Continue in this manner, attaching a coral piece after every fourth net segment, until you reach the end of the ladder. Repeat to complete the remaining half of ladder 3.

Pin all of the netted ends in place so that they are taut and evenly distributed.

Step F: Ladder 4

All Units
- 11° red seed x 1
- 6mm twisted red bugle x 1
- 11° red seed x 1

Ladder 4 will wrap around the outer points of the netting from the previous row. The first unit and the last unit will extend from the first to the last netted point.

Build ladder 4 and pin it to the template.

Sew through the first unit of ladder 4, exiting the inside edge, and then through the 11° black seed at the bottom center of the first net. Sew through the next unit, exiting the outside edge. Weave in and out through the ladder until you reach the next netted point. Sew through this point. Continue to the end of the ladder, joining net points as you reach them.

Step G: Ladder 5

All Units
- 11° red seed x 1
- 6mm untwisted red bugle x 1
- 11° red seed x 1

Build ladder 5 and pin it to the template.

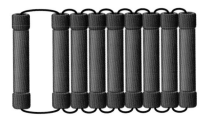

Step H: Bottom Picots and Surface Embellishment

Begin at the center of ladder 5 and work from left to right. Find the two bead units nearest to the halfway point. Sew through the first of the two units, exiting the outside of ladder 5.

Pick up one 8° red seed and one 11° black seed. Skip the black seed and sew through the red one and then through the second bead unit of the two-unit group, exiting the inside of ladder 5.

Pick up one coral piece and one 11° red seed. Sew back through the coral piece and down through the next bead unit. Weave up, down, up, and down through the next four bead units and make another picot.

Continue in this manner, attaching a coral piece after every picot, until you reach the end of the ladder. Repeat to complete the remaining half of ladder 3.

Step I: Finishing

Add a closure to the open ends of the neckpiece. Weave in the thread ends. Attach a clasp. If necessary, refer to the finishing technique instructions on pages 30–32.

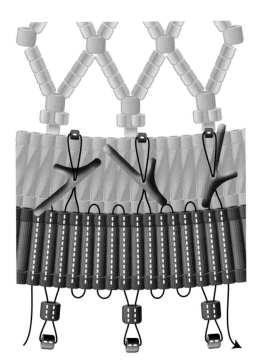

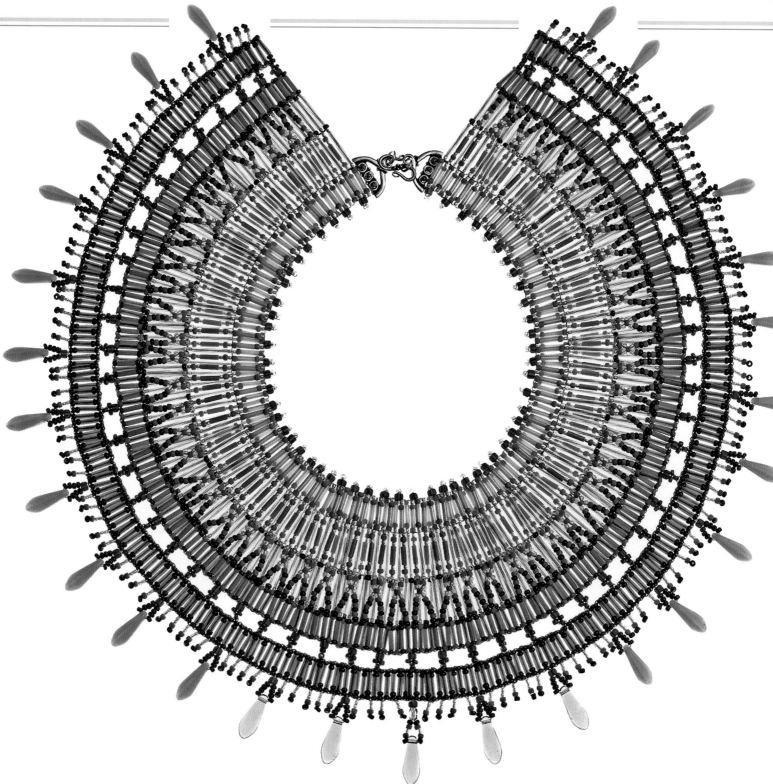

Spike

This striking collar combines layering and spiked fringe.

BEAD KEY

12mm twisted,
chartreuse bugles
size A = 27 g; size B = 13 g;
size C = 36 g

6mm untwisted,
dark turquoise bugles
size A = 17 g; size B = 19 g;
size C = 21 g

6mm untwisted,
light turquoise bugles
size A = 9 g; size B = 11 g;
size C = 12 g

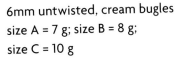

6mm untwisted, cream bugles
size A = 7 g; size B = 8 g;
size C = 10 g

11° dark turqoise seeds
size A = 25 g; size B = 28 g; size C = 31 g

11° light turquoise seeds
size A = 21 g; size B = 24 g; size C = 27 g

11° white seeds
size A = 20 g; size B = 24 g; size C = 27 g

8° dark turquoise seeds
size A = 5 g; size B = 5 g; size C = 6 g

Large turquoise and
chartreuse daggers
size A = 39; size B = 44; size C = 49

Step A: Ladder 1

Unit 1 (top to bottom)

• 11° white seed x 1
• 11° light turquoise seed x 1
• 6mm untwisted white bugle x 1
• 11° light turquoise seed x 1

Unit 2 (bottom to top)

• 11° white seed x 1
• 11° light turquoise seed x 1
• 6mm untwisted white bugle x 1
• 11° light turquoise seed x 1

Build ladder 1 and pin it to the template.

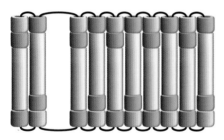

Step B: Ladder 2 and Inside Picots

Unit 1 (top to bottom)

• 11° white seed x 1
• 12mm twisted chartreuse bugle x 1
• 11° white seed x 1

Unit 2 (bottom to top)

• 11° white seed x 1
• 11° light turquoise seed x 1
• 11° white seed x 1
• 6mm untwisted light turquoise bugle x 1
• 11° white seed x 1
• 11° light turquoise seed x 1
• 11° white seed x 1

Build ladder 2 and pin it to the template.

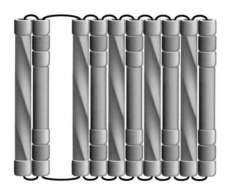

Join ladder 1 and ladder 2. Every other time that you exit the inside of ladder 1, pick up one 8° dark turquoise seed and one 11° white seed. Sew back through the 8° dark turquoise seed and then through the next bead unit to complete a picot.

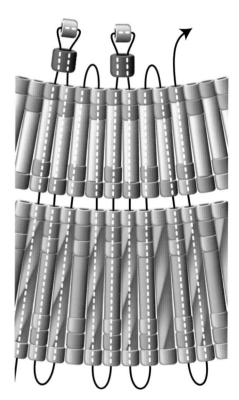

Step C: Ladder 3

Unit 1 (top to bottom)

• 11° dark turquoise seed x 1
• 12mm twisted chartreuse bugle x 1
• 11° white seed x 1

Unit 2 (bottom to top)

• 11° dark turquoise seed x 1
• 12mm twisted chartreuse bugle x 1
• 11° white seed x 1

Build ladder 3 and pin it to the template. Join ladder 2 and ladder 3.

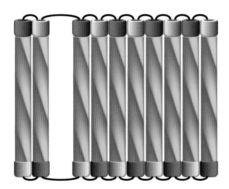

Step D: Ladder 4

Unit 1 (top to bottom)

• 11° light turquoise seed x 1
• 6mm untwisted dark turquoise bugle x 1
• 11° light turquoise seed x 1

Unit 2 (bottom to top)

• 11° dark turquoise seed x 1
• 6mm untwisted light turquoise bugle x 1
• 11° dark turquoise seed x 1

Build ladder 3 and pin it to the template. Join ladder 3 and ladder 4.

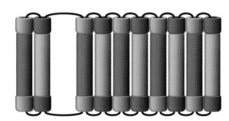

Step E: Net Overlay and Outside Picots

This netting spans from the inside of ladder 4 to the outside of ladder 2, overlaying ladder 3.

Begin at the center of ladder 4 and work from left to right. Find the unit nearest to the halfway point. Count two units outward on both sides for a total of five bead units. Sew through the first unit of the five units, exiting the inside of ladder 4.

Pick up:

- 11° dark turquoise seed x 1
- 11° light turquoise seed x 1
- 11° dark turquoise seed x 1
- 11° light turquoise seed x 1
- 11° dark turquoise seed x 1
- 11° light turquoise seed x 1
- 11° white seed x 1
- 11° light turquoise seed x 1
- 11° white seed x 1
- 11° light turquoise seed x 1
- 11° white seed x 1

Make a ray to the center of the template by extending a length of thread from the center of ladder 4's five-bead unit to the center point of the template. For the first net, this

ray will be on the vertical center-line of the template. Find the two units of ladder 2 that are closest to the ray and sew through first unit, exiting the inside of the ladder. Sew through the next unit, exiting the outside of the ladder.

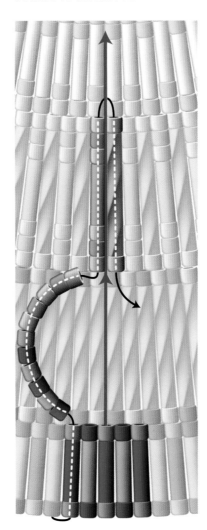

Pick up:

- 11° white seed x 1
- 11° light turquoise seed x 1
- 11° white seed x 1

Sew down through the fourth bead from the top, making sure not to split the thread.

Pick up:

- 11° white seed x 1
- 11° light turquoise seed x 1
- 11° dark turquoise seed x 1
- 11° light turquoise seed x 1
- 11° dark turquoise seed x 1
- 11° light turquoise seed x 1
- 11° dark turquoise seed x 1

Skip three bead units and sew through the last of the five units, exiting the outside of ladder 4.

Pick up one 8° dark turquoise seed and three 11° dark turquoise seeds. Skip the last three beads and sew back through the 8° dark turquoise seed to complete a picot and then up through the next unit, exiting the inside of ladder 4. Begin a new net and repeat this process, making netting and picots, to the end of the ladder. Tie off the thread and then work in the opposite direction with the tail thread.

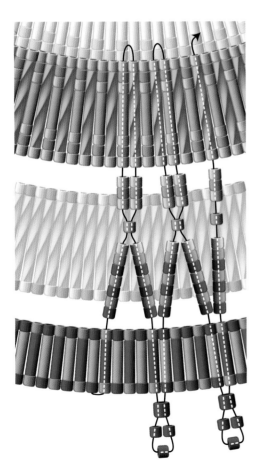

Step F: Ladder 5

Unit 1 (top to bottom)

- 11° dark turquoise seeds x 2
- 6mm untwisted dark turquoise bugle x 1
- 11° dark turquoise seed x 1

Unit 2 (bottom to top)

- 11° dark turquoise seeds x 2
- 6mm untwisted dark turquoise bugle x 1
- 11° dark turquoise seed x 1

Build ladder 3 and pin it to the template.

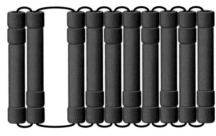

Sew through the first unit of ladder 5, exiting the inside edge, and then through the center bead of the first picot. Sew through the next unit, exiting the outside edge. Weave in and out through the ladder until you reach the next picot. Sew through the center bead. Continue to the end of the ladder, joining picot points as you reach them.

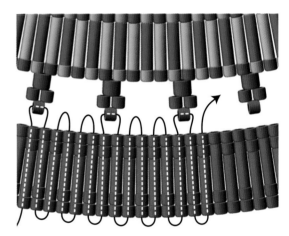

Step G: Fringe and Daggers

Begin at the center of ladder 5 and work from left to right. Find the two units nearest to the vertical centerline. Sew through the unit to the left, exiting the outside of ladder 5.

This neckpiece has two types of fringe—dagger fringe and short fringe.

For the dagger fringe, pick up:

• 8° dark turquoise seed x 1
• 11° dark turquoise seeds x 4
• large dagger bead x 1
• 11° dark turquoise seeds x 4

Optional: Make the center fringe stand out by substituting the above with this sequence:

• 8° dark turquoise seed x 1
• 4mm green crystal bead x 1
• 11° dark turquoise seed x 1
• 11° light turquoise seed x 1
• 11° white seed x 1
• large dagger bead x 1
• 11° white seed x 1
• 11° light turquoise seed x 1
• 11° dark turquoise seed x 1

Sew back through the size 8 dark turquoise seed (and the crystal as well if using the above sequence). Sew back through the next unit of ladder 5, exiting the inside edge of the ladder.

For the short fringe, pick up:

• 11° white seeds x 2
• 11° light turquoise seed x 1
• 11° dark turquoise seed x 1

Skip the last seed and sew through the strand. Sew back through the next unit of ladder 5, exiting the inside of the ladder.

Make five short fringes between every dagger fringe. Continue to both ends of the ladder. Tie off the thread.

Step H: Finishing

Add a closure to the open ends of the neckpiece. Weave in the thread ends. Attach a clasp. If necessary, refer to the finishing technique instructions on pages 30-32.

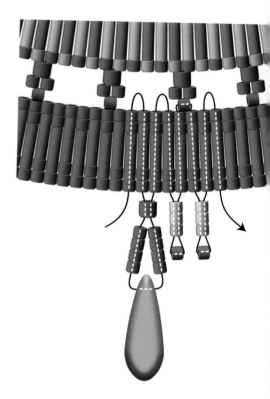

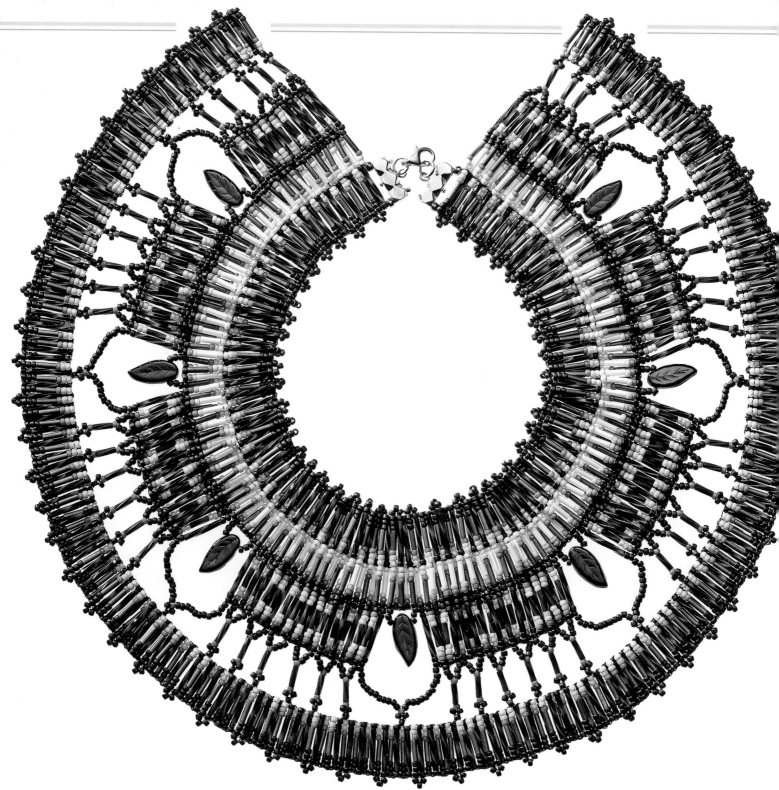

Gradient

Gradual color changes and dangling leaves give this unusual piece its unique style.

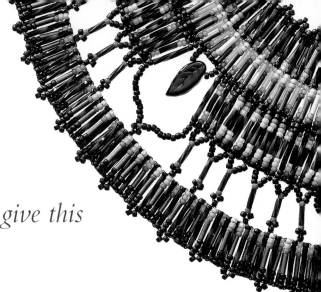

BEAD KEY

12mm twisted black bugles
size A = 28 g; size B = 33 g;
size C = 37 g

6mm twisted black bugles
size A = 7 g; size B = 8 g;
size C = 9 g

6mm untwisted dark gray bugles
size A = 14 g; size B = 16 g;
size C = 18 g

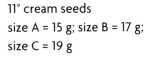

6mm untwisted cream bugles
size A = 4 g; size B = 5 g;
size C = 6 g

11° black seeds
size A = 31 g; size B = 37 g; size C = 41 g

11° medium gray seeds
size A = 10 g; size B = 12 g; size C = 13 g

11° light gray seeds
size A = 9 g; size B = 10 g; size C = 11 g

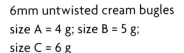

11° cream seeds
size A = 15 g; size B = 17 g;
size C = 19 g

15mm flat black leaves, with horizontal hole (7)

Step A: Ladder 1

Unit 1 (top to bottom)

- 11° black seeds x 3
- 6mm untwisted black bugle x 1
- 11° medium gray seed x 1
- 11° light gray seed x 1
- 11° cream seed x 1

Unit 2 (bottom to top)

- 11° black seed x 1
- 12mm twisted black bugle x 1
- 11° black seed x 1

Build ladder 1 and pin it to the template.

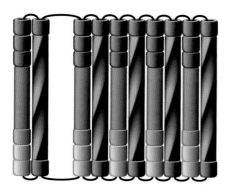

Step B: Ladder 2 and Top Picots

Unit 1 (top to bottom)

- 11° cream seed x 1
- 11° light gray seed x 1
- 11° medium gray seed x 1
- 6mm untwisted black bugle x 1
- 11° black seed x 1

Unit 2 (bottom to top)

- 11° black seed x 1
- 11° medium gray seed x 1
- 11° light gray seed x 1
- 6mm untwisted cream bugle x 1
- 11° cream seed x 1

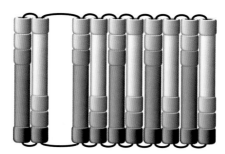

Build ladder 2 and pin it to the template. Join ladder 1 and ladder 2. Every other time that you exit the inside edge of ladder 1, string three 11° black seeds to form a picot.

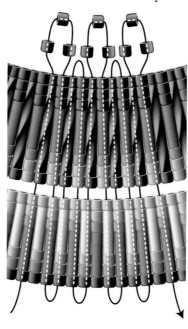

Step C: Ladder 3 and Leaf Drops

Unit 1 (top to bottom)

- 11° black seeds x 2
- 12mm twisted black bugle x 1
- 11° black seeds x 2

Unit 2 (bottom to top)

- 11° black seed x 1
- 11° medium gray seed x 1
- 11° light gray seed x 1
- 11° cream seed x 1
- 6mm twisted black bugle x 1
- 11° cream seed x 1
- 11° light gray seed x 1
- 11° medium gray seed x 1
- 11° black seed x 1

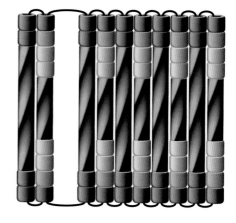

Unlike the first two ladders, ladder 3 has eight separate ladder segments. To find the correct length of each segment, locate each of the ⅛ lines on your template (not counting the top center line). Find the bead unit of ladder 2 nearest to each line. Count three units outward on each side for a total of seven bead units. Mark these units on the template.

Make a ladder segment of the appropriate length to extend from the last bead unit of a seven-unit group to the first bead unit of the next seven-unit group. Count the number of bead units in this ladder segment and make five more identical segments.

The two end segments will span from the last bead unit of a seven-unit group to each of the end units of ladder 2. Pin each ladder segment to the template. Make sure that there are five exposed bead units of ladder 2 at each ⅛ line.

Join the first segment of ladder 3 to ladder 2. Ideally, your needle will be positioned so that it exits the first of the five exposed bead units at the outside edge of ladder 2 to begin the leaf segment. If not, work around until you can exit the correct unit.

Pick up:
- 11° black seeds x 3
- 15mm flat black leaf x 1
- 11° black seeds x 3

Sew through the last bead unit of the five-unit group, exiting the inside edge of ladder 2. Sew through the next unit and begin to join the next segment of ladder 3. Repeat this process until you have joined all eight ladder sections and added all seven leaf beads.

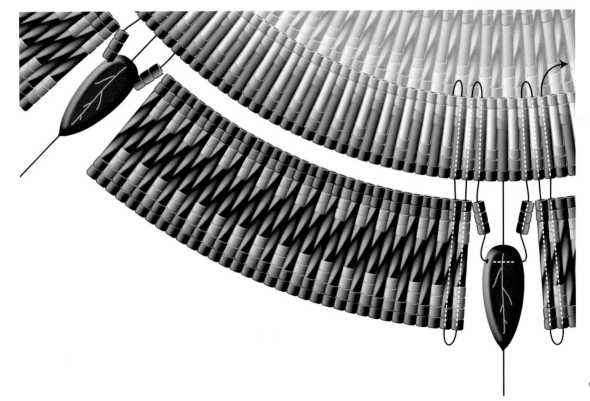

Step D: Netted Spokes

For this design, you will add netted spokes to the outside edge of the segments of ladder 3. You'll also add a larger net span between segments. Each net will occupy a four-unit group, with an extra unit on either end of each segment to accommodate the larger net span. So you'll need to work with a multiple of four units for each spoke and one extra unit on each end of the ladder segment (4 + 2).

The actual ladder segment will vary in length (and number of bead units), depending on the size of the neckpiece. You always need a free unit on each end, but depending on the size of the segment, you may need to make some adjustments. If so, here are some guidelines.

If your ladder segment consists of a multiple of 4 + 0 extra units, two of the netted spokes (preferably at the ends of the segment) will occupy a five-unit group.

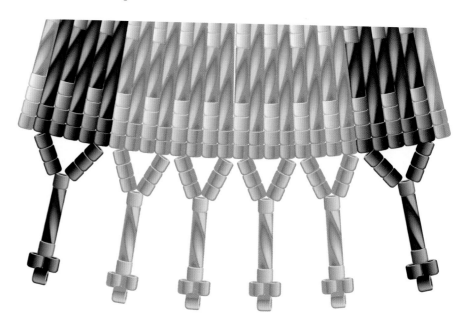

If your ladder segment consists of a multiple of 4 + 1 extra unit, one of the netted spokes (preferably in the middle of the segment) will occupy a three-unit group.

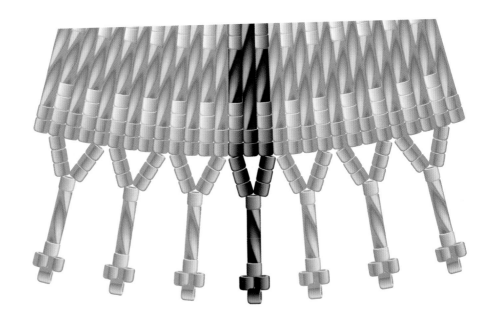

If your ladder segment consists of a multiple of 4 + 3 extra units, one of the netted spokes (preferably in the middle of the segment) will occupy a five-unit group.

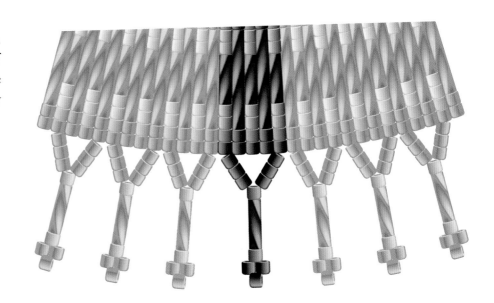

Sew through the last bead unit to the left of the halfway line, exiting the outside edge of ladder 3.

Pick up:

- 11° black seeds x 12
- 11° medium gray seed x 1
- 11° black seeds x 3

Skip the last three beads and sew through the 11° medium gray seed. Pick up twelve 11° black seeds and sew up through the first bead unit of the next ladder segment, exiting the inside edge. Sew through the next bead unit of ladder 3, exiting the outside edge.

Pick up:

- 11° black seeds x 3
- 11° medium gray seed x 1
- 6mm twisted black bugle x 1
- 11° black seeds x 3

Skip the last three beads and sew through the next three beads. Pick up three 11° black seeds and sew up through last unit of the four-unit group (take into account any adjustments you've made in the ladder segment), exiting the inside edge. Sew through the next bead unit of ladder 3, exiting the outside edge. Add netted spikes to the remainder of the ladder.

Continue this process until you reach the end of ladder 3, adding netted spikes and nets that extend from one ladder segment to the next. Complete the remaining half of the ladder. Pin all of the netted ends in place so that they are taut and evenly distributed.

Step E: Ladder 4

Ladder 4 will wrap around the outer points of the netting from the previous row. The first unit and the last unit will extend from the first to the last netted point.

Unit 1 (top to bottom)

- 11° cream seed x 1
- 11° light gray seed x 1
- 11° medium gray seed x 1
- 6mm untwisted black bugle x 1
- 11° black seeds x 3

Unit 2 (bottom to top)

- 11° black seed x 1
- 12mm twisted black bugle x 1
- 11° black seed x 1

Build ladder 4 and pin it to the template.

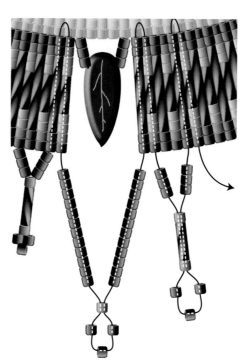

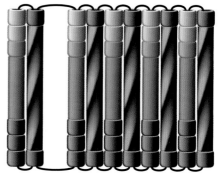

Sew through the first unit of ladder 4, exiting the inside edge, and then through the 11° black seed at the bottom center of the first net. Sew through the next unit, exiting the outside edge. Weave in and out through the ladder until you reach the next netted point. Sew through this point. Continue to the end of the ladder, joining net points as you reach them.

Step F: Bottom Picots

Begin at the center of ladder 3 and work from left to right. Find the two bead units nearest to the halfway point. Sew through the first of the two units, exiting the outside of ladder 4. Pick up three 11° black seeds and sew up, down, up, down, up, down through the next six bead units. Begin the next picot.

Continue this process to the end of ladder 3. Complete the remaining half of the ladder.

Step G: Finishing

Add a closure to the open ends of the neckpiece. Weave in the thread ends. Attach a clasp. If necessary, refer to the finishing technique instructions on pages 30–32.

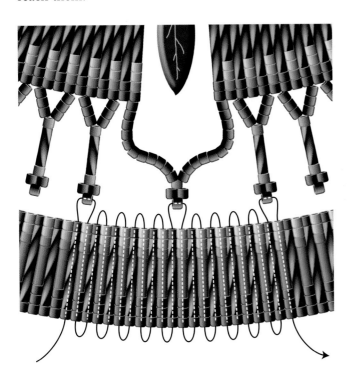

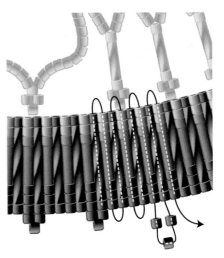

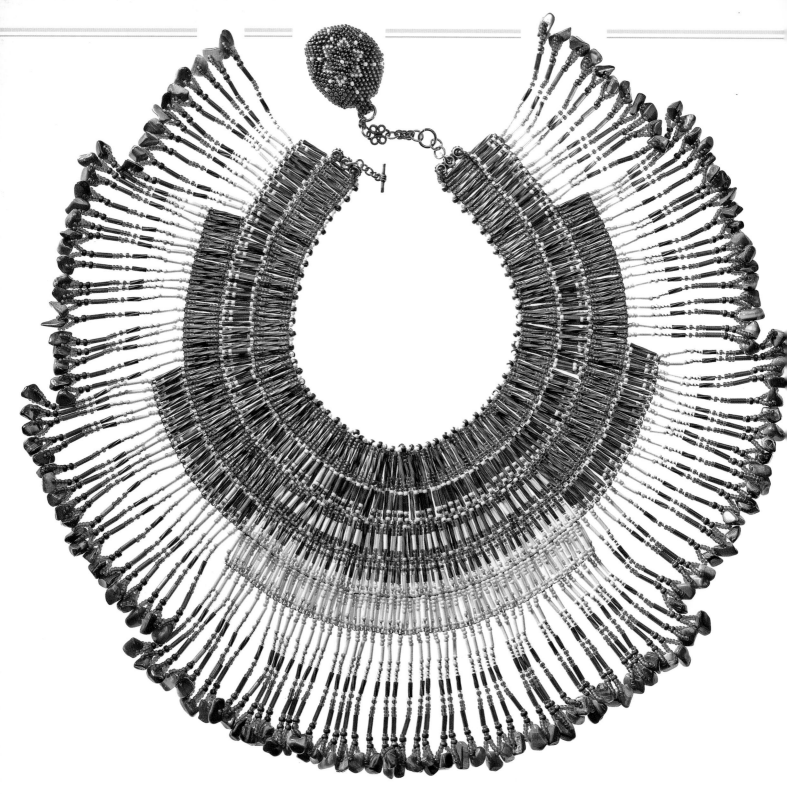

Eagle Feather

Inspired by Native American imagery, this neckpiece is built with multiple ladders and dense fringe.

BEAD KEY

12mm twisted iridescent blue bugles
size A = 28 g; size B = 33 g;
size C = 38 g

6mm twisted iridescent blue bugles
size A = 13 g; size B = 15 g;
size C = 17 g

6mm untwisted brown bugles
size A = 11 g; size B = 12 g;
size C = 14 g

6mm untwisted cream bugles
size A = 11 g; size B = 12 g;
size C = 14 g

11° brown seeds
size A = 49 g; size B = 57 g;
size C = 65 g

11° pale blue seeds
size A = 16 g; size B = 19 g;
size C = 21 g

11° cream seeds
size A = 23 g; size B = 26 g;
size C = 29 g

8° purple seeds
size A = 12 g; size B = 13 g;
size C = 15 g

Tigereye nuggets
size A = 147; size B = 204;
size C = 229

Step A: Ladder 1

Unit 1 (top to bottom)

- 11° brown seed x 1
- 12mm twisted iridescent blue bugle x 1
- 11° brown seed x 1

Unit 2 (bottom to top)

- 11° brown seeds x 3
- 6mm twisted iridescent blue bugle x 1
- 11° brown seeds x 3

Build ladder 1 and pin it to the template.

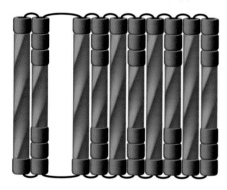

Step B: Top Picots

Begin at the center of ladder 1 and work from left to right. Find the unit nearest to the halfway point. Count one unit outward on both sides for a total of three bead units. Sew through the first of the three units, exiting the inside of ladder 1.

Pick up:

- 11° cream seed x 1
- 8° purple seed x 1
- 11° cream seed x 1

Sew through the third unit of the three-unit group, exiting the outside edge. Sew through the next unit and begin a new picot. Repeat until you reach the end of ladder 1. Complete the remaining half of the ladder.

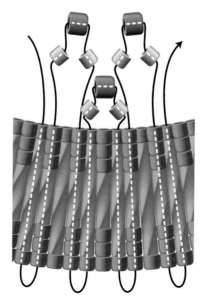

Step C: Ladder 2

Unit 1 (top to bottom)

11° pale blue seed x 1

12mm twisted iridescent blue bugle x 1

11° pale blue seed x 1

Unit 2 (bottom to top)

- 11° brown seed x 1
- 11° cream seed x 1
- 11° brown seed x 1
- 11° cream seed x 1
- 6mm untwisted brown bugle x 1
- 11° cream seed x 1
- 11° brown seed x 1

Build ladder 2 and pin it to the template. Join ladder 1 and ladder 2.

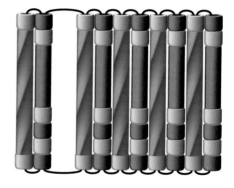

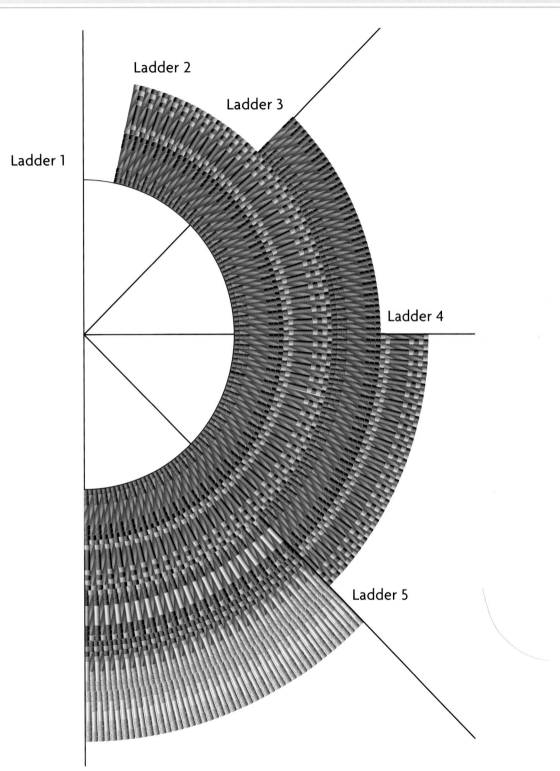

Ladder 1

Ladder 2

Ladder 3

Ladder 4

Ladder 5

Step D: Ladder 3

Ladder 3 will begin and end at each of the ⅛ lines on your template. The ladder is made up of three connected segments.

Ladder Segment 1

(⅛ line to ⅜ line)

Unit 1 (top to bottom)

- 11° brown seed x 1
- 12mm twisted iridescent blue bugle x 1
- 11° brown seed x 1

Unit 2 (bottom to top)

- 11° brown seeds x 3
- 6mm twisted iridescent blue bugle x 1
- 11° brown seeds x 3

Build ladder segment 1. Stop when you reach the ⅜ line on your template. Do not end the thread. Continue by picking up the bead-unit sequence for ladder segment 2.

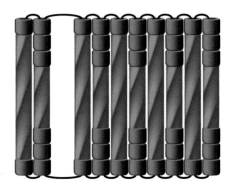

Ladder Segment 2

(⅜ line to ⅜ line)

Unit 1 (top to bottom)

- 11° brown seeds x 3
- 6mm untwisted cream bugle x 1
- 11° brown seeds x 3

Unit 2 (bottom to top)

- 11° cream seed x 1
- 12mm twisted iridescent blue bugle x 1
- 11° cream seed x 1

Build ladder segment 2. Stop when you reach the next ⅜ line. Do not end the thread. Continue by picking up the bead-unit sequence for ladder segment 3.

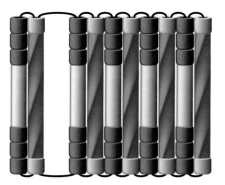

Ladder Segment 3

(⅜ line to ⅛ line)

Unit 1 (top to bottom)

- 11° brown seed x 1
- 12mm twisted iridescent blue bugle x 1
- 11° brown seed x 1

Unit 2 (bottom to top)

- 11° brown seeds x 3
- 6mm twisted iridescent blue bugle x 1
- 11° brown seeds x 3

Build ladder segment 3. Stop when you reach the ⅛ line. Pin ladder 3 to the template so that it reaches from one ⅛ line to the other. Join ladder 2 and ladder 3.

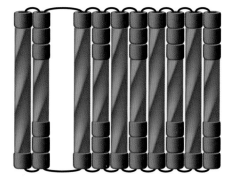

Step E: Ladder 4

Ladder 4 will begin and end at ¼ lines. It is made up of three connected segments.

Ladder Segment 1

(¼ line to ⅜ line)

Unit 1 (top to bottom)

- 11° pale blue seed x 1
- 12mm twisted iridescent blue bugle x 1
- 11° pale blue seed x 1

Unit 2 (bottom to top)

- 11° brown seed x 1
- 11° cream seed x 1
- 11° brown seed x 1
- 11° cream seed x 1
- 6mm untwisted brown bugle x 1
- 11° cream seed x 1
- 11° brown seed x 1

Build ladder segment 1. Stop when it reaches the ⅜ line. Do not end the thread. Continue by picking up the bead-unit sequence for ladder segment 2.

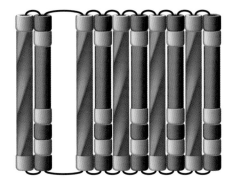

Ladder Segment 2

(⅜ line to ⅜ line)

Unit 1 (top to bottom)

- 11° brown seed x 1
- 11° pale blue seed x 1
- 11° brown seed x 1
- 11° pale blue seed x 1
- 6mm untwisted cream bugle x 1
- 11° cream seeds x 2

Unit 2 (bottom to top)

- 11° cream seed x 1
- 11° pale blue seed x 1
- 11° cream seed x 1
- 11° pale blue seed x 1
- 6mm twisted iridescent blue bugle x 1
- 11° brown seeds x 2

Build ladder segment 2. Stop when you reach the next ⅜ line. Do not end the thread. Continue by picking up the bead-unit sequence for ladder segment 3.

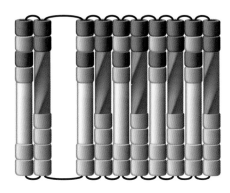

Ladder Segment 3

(⅜ line to ¼ line)

Unit 1 (top to bottom)

- 11° pale blue seed x 1
- 12mm twisted iridescent blue bugle x 1
- 11° pale blue seed x 1

Unit 2 (bottom to top)

- 11° brown seed x 1
- 11° cream seed x 1
- 11° brown seed x 1
- 11° cream seed x 1
- 6mm untwisted brown bugle x 1
- 11° cream seed x 1
- 11° brown seed x 1

Build ladder segment 3. Stop when it reaches the ¼ line. Pin ladder 4 to the template so that it reaches from one ¼ line to the other. Join ladder 3 and ladder 4.

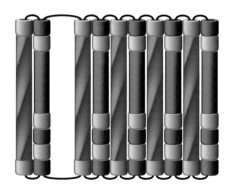

Step F: Ladder 5

Ladder 5 will begin and end at each of the ⅜ lines.

Unit 1 (top to bottom)

• 11° cream seeds x 4
• 6mm untwisted cream bugle x 1
• 11° cream seeds x 2

Unit 2 (bottom to top)

• 11° pale blue seed x 1
• 11° cream seed x 1
• 11° pale blue seed x 1
• 11° cream seed x 1
• 6mm untwisted cream bugle x 1
• 11° cream seeds x 2

Pin ladder 5 to the template so that it reaches from one ⅜ line to the other. Join ladder 4 and ladder 5.

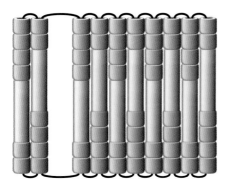

Step G: Fringe

Begin at the center of ladder 5 and work from left to right. Find the two units nearest to the halfway point. Sew through the unit first of the two units, exiting the outside of ladder 5.

Pick up:

• 11° cream seeds x 3
• 6mm untwisted cream bugle x 1
• 11° cream seed x 1
• 11° pale blue seed x 1
• 11° cream seed x 1
• 11° pale blue seeds x 3
• 6mm twisted iridescent blue bugle x 1
• 11° pale blue seed x 1
• 11° brown seed x 1
• 11° pale blue seed x 1
• 11° brown seeds x 3
• 6mm untwisted brown bugle x 1
• 11° brown seed x 1
• 8° purple seed x 1
• 11° brown seed x 1
• 8° purple seed x 1
• 11° brown seeds x 5
• tigereye nugget x 1
• 11° brown seeds x 5

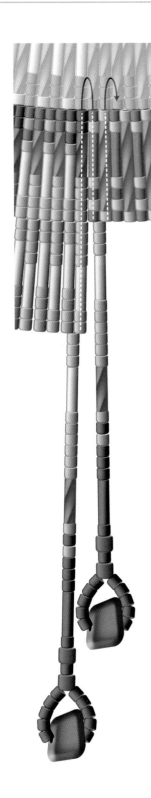

Skip the last eleven beads. Sew up through the remainder of the strand and then through the second bead unit in the two-unit group, exiting the inside edge. Sew through the next bead unit and begin another fringe strand.

Work to the end of ladder 5. If you end on an odd-numbered bead unit, simply complete the last strand of fringe and sew back up through the same unit that you exited.

Sew up through the adjoining bead unit of ladder 4, exiting the inside edge. Sew back through the next bead unit, exiting the outside edge, and begin a new fringe strand.

Repeat to the end of the neckpiece. Complete the remaining half.

Step E: Finishing

Add a closure to the open ends of the neckpiece. Weave in the thread ends. Attach a clasp. If necessary, refer to the finishing technique instructions on pages 30–32.

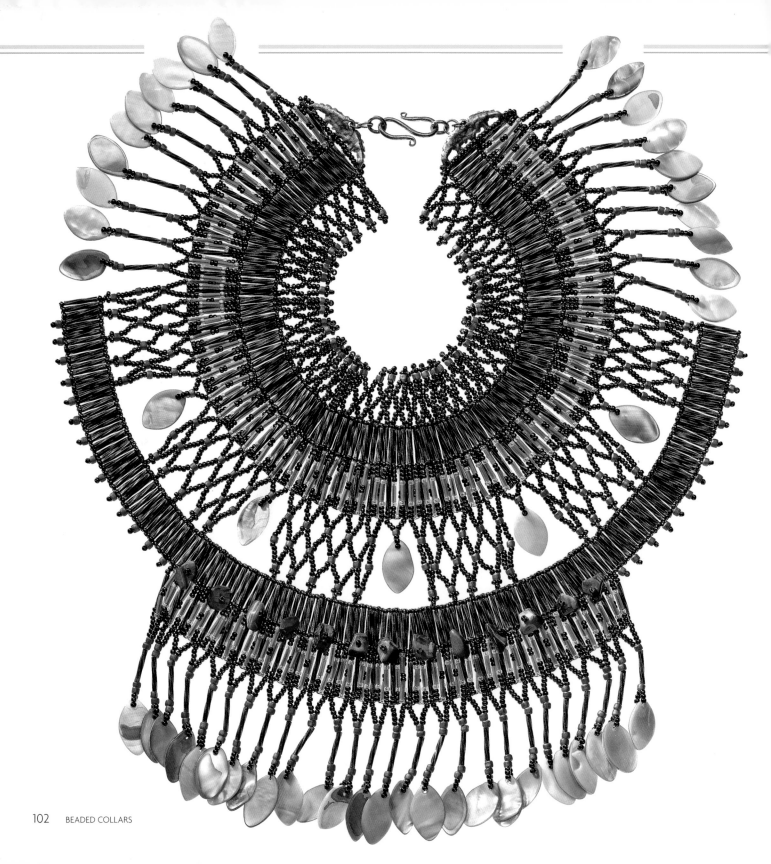

Trellis

This fascinating collar features sectioned netting and tiered fringe.

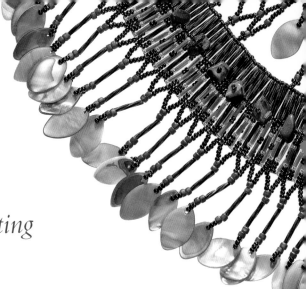

BEAD KEY

12mm twisted bronze bugles
size A = 39 g; size B = 46 g;
size C = 52 g

6mm untwisted dark
turquoise bugles
size A = 12 g; size B = 14 g;
size C = 16 g

11° bronze seeds
size A = 59 g; size B = 69 g;
size C = 79 g

11° pale green seeds
size A = 6 g; size B = 7 g; size C = 8 g

8° dark turquoise seeds
size A = 11 g; size B = 13 g; size C = 14 g

Tigereye nuggets
size A = 13; size B = 21; size C = 23

20mm flat mother-of-pearl drops,
with front-to-back hole
size A = 51; size B = 80; size C = 90

Step A: Ladder 1

All Units

- 11° bronze seed x 1
- 12mm twisted bronze bugle x 1
- 11° bronze seed x 1

Build ladder 1 and pin it to the template.

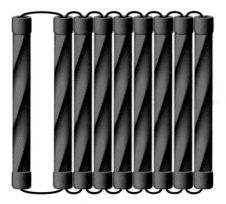

Step B: Top Netting

Begin at the center of ladder 1 and work from left to right. Find the two units nearest to the halfway point and count outward by one unit on each side for a total of four units. Sew through the first unit of the four units, exiting the inside of ladder 1.

Pick up:

- 11° bronze seeds x 11
- 8° dark turquoise seed x 1
- 11° bronze seeds x 3

Skip the last three beads and sew through the 8° dark turquoise seed. Pick up seven 11° bronze seeds. Skip the next seven beads and sew through the eighth bead. Pick up three 11° bronze seeds and sew through the last bead unit in the four-unit group. Sew up through the next bead unit, exiting the inside edge of ladder 1, to begin the next net segment.

Pick up seven 11° bronze seeds. Skip the first seven beads of the first netted segment and sew through the next bead.

Pick up:

- 11° bronze seeds x 3
- 8° dark turquoise seed x 1
- 11° bronze seeds x 3

Complete this net segment as you did the first. Repeat to the end of ladder 1. Complete the remaining half of the ladder.

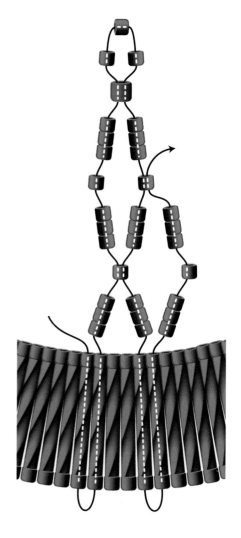

Step C: Ladder 2

Unit 1 (top to bottom)

- 11° bronze seed x 2
- 12mm twisted bronze bugle x 1
- 11° bronze seed x 2

Unit 2 (bottom to top)

- 11° bronze seeds x 3
- 11° pale green seed x 1
- 6mm untwisted dark turquoise bugle x 1
- 11° pale green seed x 1
- 11° bronze seeds x 3

Unit 3 (top to bottom)

- 11° pale green seed x 1
- 6mm untwisted dark turquoise bugle x 1
- 11° bronze seeds x 2
- 6mm untwisted dark turquoise bugle x 1
- 11° pale green seed x 1

Unit 4 (bottom to top)

- 11° bronze seeds x 3
- 11° pale green seed x 1
- 6mm untwisted dark turquoise bugle x 1
- 11° pale green seed x 1
- 11° bronze seeds x 3

Build ladder 1 and pin it to the template. Join ladder 1 and ladder 2.

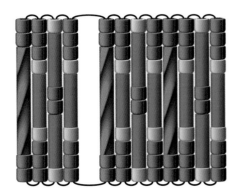

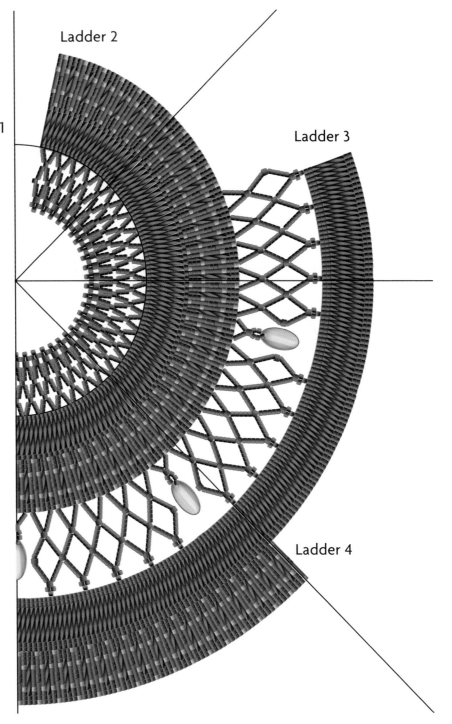

Step D: Netting and Drops

Begin at the center of ladder 1 and work from left to right. Find the unit nearest the halfway point. Count outward by two units on each side for a total of five units. Sew through the first of the five units, exiting the outside of ladder 2.

Pick up:

- 11° bronze seeds x 3
- 8° dark turquoise seed x 1
- 11° bronze seeds x 3
- 20mm flat mother-of-pearl drop x 1
- 11° bronze seeds x 3

Skip the next seven beads and sew up through the 8° dark turquoise bead. Pick up three 11° bronze seeds. Sew through the last bead unit of the five-unit group. The drop should straddle the center unit.

Sew through the next bead unit, exiting the outside edge of ladder 2. Each segment of netting will span a five-unit group.

Pick up:

- 11° bronze seeds x 5
- 8° dark turquoise seed x 1
- 11° bronze seeds x 5
- 8° dark turquoise seed x 1
- 11° bronze seeds x 5
- 8° dark turquoise seed x 1
- 11° bronze seeds x 3

Skip the last three beads and sew through the 8° dark turquoise seed.

Pick up:

- 11° bronze seeds x 5
- 8° dark turquoise seed x 1
- 11° bronze seeds x 5

Skip the next eleven beads and sew through the 8° dark turquoise seed. Pick up five 11° bronze seeds and sew through the last bead unit of the five-unit group. Sew through the next unit, exiting the outside edge of ladder 2, to begin the next net segment.

Pick up:

- 11° bronze seeds x 5
- 8° dark turquoise seed x 1
- 11° bronze seeds x 5

Skip the first eleven beads of the first net segment and go through the next 8° dark turquoise seed.

Pick up:

- 11° bronze seeds x 5
- 8° dark turquoise seed x 1
- 11° bronze seeds x 3

Complete this net segment as you did the last. Repeat until you have completed five full nets (each net will terminate with a three-bead picot).

Repeat this entire process, alternating drop and netting, until you reach the ¼ line. If necessary, work beyond this line until the last five-net section is complete. Bead the remaining half of ladder 2 in the same way.

Pin all of the netted ends in place so that they are taut and evenly distributed.

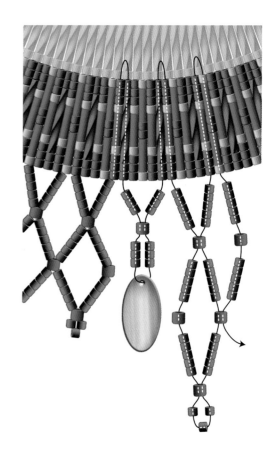

Step E: Ladder 3

All Units

- 11° bronze seed x 1
- 12mm twisted bronze bugle x 1
- 11° bronze seed x 1

Ladder 3 will wrap around the outer points of the netting from the previous row. The first unit and the last unit will extend from the first to the last netted point.

Build ladder 3 and pin it to the template.

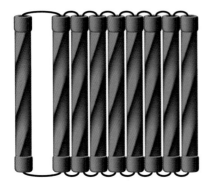

Sew through the first unit of ladder 3, exiting the inside edge, and then through the 11° brown seed at the bottom center of the first net. Sew through the next unit, exiting the outside edge. Weave in and out through the ladder until you reach the next netted point. Sew through this point. Continue to the end of the ladder, joining net points as you reach them.

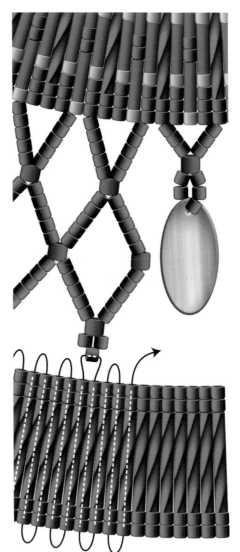

Step F: Ladder 4

Ladder 4 will extend from one ⅜ line to the other ⅜ line.

Unit 1 (top to bottom)

- 11° bronze seeds x 2
- 12mm twisted bronze bugle x 1
- 11° bronze seeds x 2

Unit 2 (bottom to top)

- 11° bronze seeds x 3
- 11° pale green seed x 1
- 6mm untwisted dark turquoise bugle x 1
- 11° pale green seed x 1
- 11° bronze seeds x 3

Unit 3 (top to bottom)

- 11° pale green seed x 1
- 6mm untwisted dark turquoise bugle x 1
- 11° bronze seeds x 2
- 6mm untwisted dark turquoise bugle x 1
- 11° pale green seed x 1

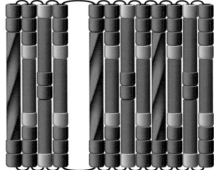

Unit 4 (bottom to top)

- 11° bronze seeds x 3
- 11° pale green seed x 1
- 6mm untwisted dark turquoise bugle x 1
- 11° pale green seed x 1
- 11° bronze seeds x 3

Build ladder 4 and pin it to the template. Join ladder 3 and ladder 4.

Step G: Fringe, Surface Embellishment, and Picots

Begin at the center of ladder 4 and work from left to right. Find the two units nearest to the halfway point and count outward by one unit on each side for a total of four units. Sew through the first of the four units, exiting the outside of ladder 4.

Pick up:

- 11° bronze seeds x 5
- 8° dark turquoise seeds x 2
- 12mm twisted bronze bugle x 1
- 8° dark turquoise seeds x 2
- 11° bronze seeds x 3
- 20mm flat mother-of-pearl drop x 1
- 11° bronze seeds x 3

Skip the last seven beads and sew through the strand until only the first five bronze seeds remain. Pick

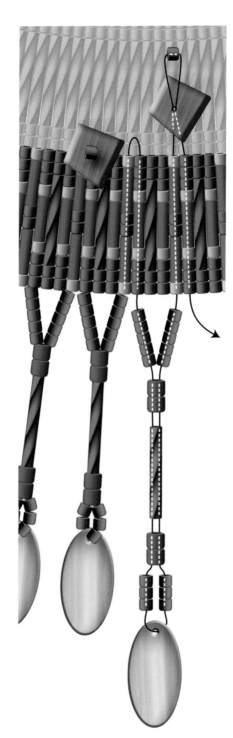

up five 11° bronze seeds and sew through the last bead unit of the four-unit group, exiting the inside edge of ladder 4.

Pick up one tigereye nugget and one 11° bronze seed. Skip the last bead and sew back through the tigereye nugget and then through the next bead unit, exiting the outside of ladder 4. Repeat to the end of ladder 4, adding surface embellishment after every other fringe strand. Don't worry if there are not enough remaining bead units to span the usual four units—simply sew up through the final unit after completing the last strand of fringe.

Sew up through the adjoining bead unit of ladder 3 and then down through the next unit to begin a series of picots. Pick up one 8° dark turquoise seed and one 11° bronze seed. Skip the last bead and sew through the 8° dark turquoise seed and then through the next bead unit, exiting the inside edge. Sew down, up, and down through the next three units and make another picot. Repeat to the end of ladder 3. Work up through the last leg of the end net and then through the adjoining unit of ladder 2. Sew back

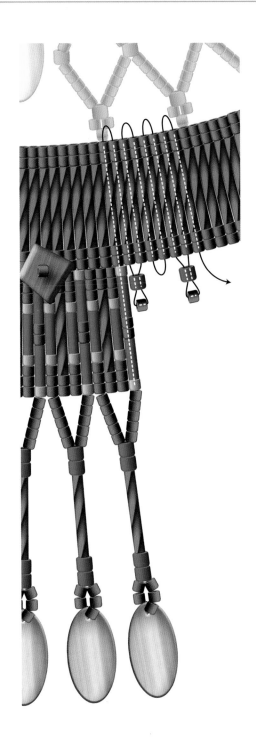

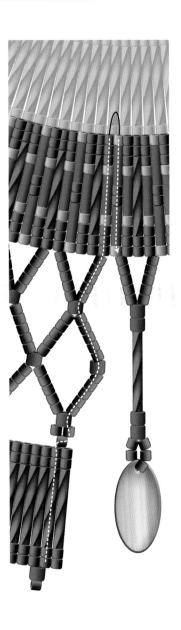

through the next unit, exiting the outside edge of ladder 2. Complete another section of fringe as you did for ladder 4, but without adding surface embellishment.

Repeat to complete the remaining half of the neckpiece.

Step H: Finishing

Add a closure to the open ends of the neckpiece. Weave in the thread ends. Attach a clasp. If necessary, refer to the finishing technique instructions on pages 30–32.

INDEX

About the Author

Julia S. Pretl is also the author of *Little Bead Boxes: 12 Miniature Boxes Built with Beads* and *Bead Knitted Bags: 10 Projects for Beaders & Knitters* (Creative Publishing international, 2006). Julia was born and raised in Baltimore, Maryland, where she still lives with her husband, Tony, and their daughters, Olive and Lily. She discovered beadwork in the late 1980s and has been beading and designing ever since. Julia enjoys spending time with her family, listening to music (rock operas are her favorite), and chatting about beads on the Internet. Visit her at www.darkharebeadwork.com.